'A mysterious, challenging and, at little more than 30,000 words, short book. But this is one book where small is beautiful. Any page of this lean, dry writing is instant transportation to the Sahara, past and present' *Traveller Magazine*

'Mixing confessional narrative, literary analysis and history, *Desert Divers* is a neat, accessible work that, for westerners drawn to the vast reaches of this desert, asks all the right questions' *New Statesman*

'*Desert Divers* is not so much a travelogue as a pilgrimage, in which colonial history illuminates literary critique, which in turn sheds light on autobiographical confession' *Independent on Sunday*

'Lindqvist's book opens up vistas as wide – and as difficult – as the desert itself' *Big Issue*

'*Desert Divers* is a powerful mix of travelogue and the history of French colonialism in North Africa. This is writing with a conscience that once again shows the enormous and provocative possibilities of the travel book' *Sunday Times*

Desert Divers

Sven Lindqvist

Translated from the Swedish by
Joan Tate

Granta Books
London · New York

Granta Publications, 2/3 Hanover Yard, London N1 8BE

First published under the title of *Ökendykarna*,
by Albert Bonniers Förlag AB, 1990
First published in Great Britain by Granta Books 2000
This edition published by Granta Books 2002

We would like to thank the Arts Council of England
for their support and assistance in this book.

A CIP catalogue record for this book
is available from the British Library.

1 3 5 7 9 10 8 6 4 2

Typeset by M Rules

Printed and bound in Great Britain
by Mackays of Chatham plc

Contents

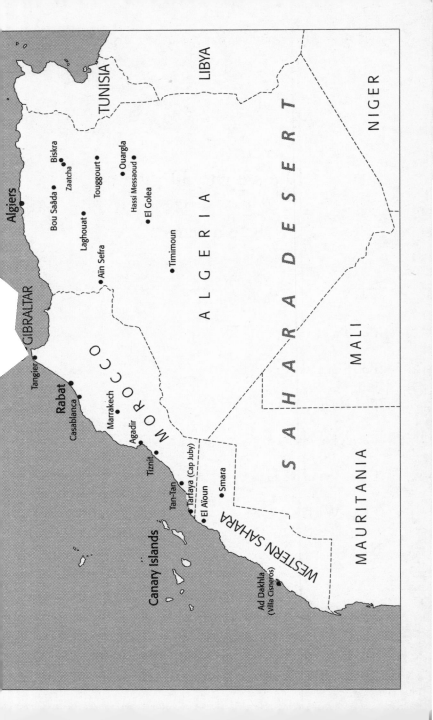

Desert Divers

To Tarfaya

1

A large muddy stone is lying in the washbasin of my hotel room.

Carefully, I scrape off the mud and rinse it. The water coming out of the tap is black.

After I have washed the stone clean, it is as pink as the morning sky. It is pink granite and made of two rounded segments resembling the halves of a brain.

Yes, now I can see it – it is my own brain which has arrived before me.

It is so heavy I can hardly lift it out of the washbasin.

2

I am woken from my dream by the usual charter-flight applause, filled with profound relief that the plane has miraculously landed in one piece at the right airport: Agadir.

Bus to the Hotel Almohades. I rent a room for the night and a car for a month.

I am not drawn to the pool, but to the desert. As a child I read about fire-eaters and well-divers, about sandstorms and desert lakes. I planned a great journey in the Sahara. Now I am here.

I am alone. I have just parted from my volumes of Dostoevsky; with all my notes in them. I have parted from the woman who was once my beloved. I have parted from thirty-three years of my life.

This has one advantage – the period of time before those thirty-three years has suddenly closed in on me.

As long as I remained in my childhood home, I could remember nothing of my childhood. It seemed to have been erased. Nothing but a bunch of anecdotes, no genuine memories.

Nor could I dream.

Now that I have moved, fragments of my childhood often come into my mind. And when I began to train with weights as I did when I was small, then I also began to dream.

Memories and dreams do not allow themselves to be forced. The very intention locks the door you want to open. You can only reach your goal by back ways and sidetracks.

One way I have tried to approach childhood several times is to do now what I so fervently longed to be allowed to do then. Even if it seems childish and unmotivated, sometimes I try what in the impotence of my smallness I dreamt of doing.

'It's like diving into black water,' says Antoine de Saint-Exupéry about a night-landing in the Sahara.

When the mail planes in his novels landed for a stopover in Agadir, the pilots had four hours before they had to go on again. I remember that as if I had read it yesterday. They went on to the town and had dinner, their bodies still singing with the vibrations of the plane.

I eat prawns au gratin at the Water Garden restaurant opposite the hotel and drink a toast to the mail plane pilots in Oulmez fizzy mineral water. Will I find that there, down south, where it really will be needed?

I am not really worried about not finding any there, but just long for it to be necessary.

At about ten in the evening on October 30, it is a little cold around the shoulders to sit outside after dinner. I go to bed early. I lie there, drawing my soul together in the no-man's-land on the borders of sleep. Then the dream interrupted on the plane comes back.

Once again I am washing that stone in black water. Bats whistle around me in the dark of the cave, the breeze from their wings waking others asleep, hanging in the roof with their heads down. Heads? The whole cave is a head, an empty skull full of a whistling darkness, in which I stand with the pink stone in my arms.

The Stravinsky-chatter of sparrows in the bush, the sky blue with light clouds. Early in the morning, I leave the monkey mountain of humanity around the hotel pool, get into my little Renault and drive slowly south.

At first the hollows are still green and glisten with moisture. The fig-cactus is just bearing fruit and bunches of ripe dates hang heavy as udders below the tops of the date palms – yellow, brown, dark red and ready to burst with the sweetness of dates.

Morocco's favourite colour is shocking pink. Instead of the white corners that we have on our red-painted houses, the houses here have reverse-stepped gables, highest in the corners and sinking towards the middle.

But soon the houses become fewer, the ground dryer. The greenery thins out until it looks like the sparse, tender green grass which grew in the sand of our Christmas crib when I was a child.

And as the desert opens up around me, as the sandy colours take over with their million monotonous variations, as the light becomes so intense that it hides shapes, extinguishes colours and flattens out levels – then my whole body hums with happiness and I feel, This is my landscape! This was where I wanted to be!

I stop the car, get out and listen.

A cricket, dark as a splinter of stone, chirps shrilly. The wind whistles in the six telephone wires, a thin, metallic note I haven't heard since childhood.

And then silence, which is even rarer.

Far away over there, the nomads' dark goat-hair tent trembles in the midday heat. Their women and children come walking in the shadow of their burdens.

5

In Tiznit, some of them have camped north of the town wall. They come from the occupied areas in the south to sell their jewellery.

They are not veiled. They have fearless children and fearless eyes. One of them is called Fatima. She has flames painted in henna on her heels, licking her foot from below.

Calmly she spreads a blue cotton cloth out on the ground. Then she starts removing objects from a little chest.

I remember Agadir's shops and their over-decorated leather goods, their rattling metal tray-tables, their thick loose mats in clashing colours – the way smoking-room orientalism has characterized the image of Morocco, perhaps the whole of North Africa.

Fatima's jewellery belongs to another, Saharan, tradition. Eagerly, I ask how much they are. She does not answer.

'This isn't the bazaar,' she admonishes me in Spanish.

I have to wait calmly as the ritual continues. Ornament after ornament is brought out and explained. 'The three tents on the lid of the box are the three tribes in Sahel.' 'This bracelet shows drought and the rains.'

Not until she has finished does she ask which objects I am interested in. She puts those into a dark wooden bowl and packs the others away in the chest.

Then she tells me which families the objects in the wooden

bowl belong to. She is selling them on their behalf. With a gentle naturalness, she gives me the prices in wheat flour.

I had imagined everything beforehand – the sandy mist in the air, the pinch of sunglasses behind my ears, the buzz of flies around military outposts, the perspiration tickling its way from armpit to waistband, everything.

But I had not imagined that only a few hours south of Agadir I would be buying Saharan ornaments for half a ton of wheat flour.

And for whom?

6

The desert road continues south along a green-floored valley.

The water supporting the greenery is nowhere to be seen but is there, beneath the ground. That is how to survive in the desert. Plants exposing themselves to evaporation have failed. The same applies to watercourses. Only those that have made their way below the surface have been able to endure.

Beside the road I see a plant with yellow flowers that leaps forward in a zigzag, covering the ground with squares like wire netting.

I see small, pale pink bell-like flowers on grey bushes and a stonecrop plant with blue star-shaped flowers and long funnels for stems.

Small cacti grow on top of one another in clumps, like coral, and protect themselves not only with spines but also with sharp milk-white juice which spurts out in all directions at the slightest touch.

To Tarfaya

For an endless half-hour I drive through a cloud of grasshoppers. They are innumerable, as large as small birds, with buzzing, transparent wings. They glisten with moisture, pink as prawns, and with the same crunching sound as when you bite into a prawn's head, they smash against the windscreen.

Something yellow and sticky is left behind and soon obscures my entire field of vision – I have to drive very slowly, until the cloud passes just as suddenly as it came.

7

Tan-Tan is a yellow town with pale blue gates. A garrison town, like Boden in the far, far north of Sweden, a disaster of a posting and where you are afflicted with their equivalent of 'Lapp sickness', *le cafard*.

The town lives off the desert war in the south. This is where the soldiers come on leave. All the small hotels are full of their families who have come to visit.

The Hotel Dakar is by the bus station. Halls and stairways are tiled, which gives an impression of cleanliness and cool. But the bathroom acoustics multiply every sound. The rooms are small and high-ceilinged. Through the closed shutters, my green room is filled with a dim aquarium light.

The sun sets at six. I sit in the twilight outside the hotel listening to the pentatonic music. The Atlantic wind is cool, almost chilly. There is no beer. The tap-water is too salty to drink. Drinking-water comes in tanker carts drawn by small tractors. I no longer long to *need* Oulmez but to drink some.

Inside the café the television blares. The video shop rents out videos. *The Terminator* is on at the cinema. Photocopiers make photocopies. The street lights come on automatically. But the waiter who had said that they have all kinds of vegetables comes back to tell me they have no cauliflower. A moment later he tells me that they have no carrots. When asked what they do have, he suggests tomatoes.

Cats roam hungrily around the table. Everyone shouts for Hasan, apparently because everyone not called Mohammed is called Hasan. When the food comes, the tomatoes, representing 'all kinds of vegetables', turn out to be purée, squeezed out of a tube over the rice.

Before I fall asleep, I see the basket of bloodstained goat hooves, which were for sale in the market. What can they be used for? Maybe to boil down for glue?

In the borderland of sleep, I smell the glue pot from the woodwork room where my father taught, the copper pot with thick layers of congealed glue stuck to its sides . . .

And the workbench from below! I am sitting down there among the sweet-smelling shavings, listening to the tearing sound of the plane, and the shavings come flying down to me, curly, rolled up – the thin fragrant skin of wood . . .

I lie curled up beneath a thick desert blanket of greasy wool. Dogs howl in the night. Perhaps my childhood has not vanished after all. It is true I have virtually not a single memory from that time, but perhaps my memory is only out of sight, like the watercourses in the desert. It has survived by disappearing from the surface and still runs in the depths, where I am heading.

8

I am buried. But I am far from helpless. Like the pea under the
princess's mattresses, I lie under layers of sediment, beneath
continents and continental plates. They are forced to shift.
My irritating presence is interrupting geological eras and
making the continents change direction.

When I get back home, I go and mangle sheets. The old-
fashioned hand-driven mangle rolls the washing between
polished marble blocks. The upper roller turns out to be the
bottom of the Atlantic on its way west to be devoured by the
mantle. Suddenly it turns right round so that Boston returns to
Casablanca and Rio to the mouth of the Congo.

I persuade myself I am still in control. But soon the move-
ments of the continents become more and more unpredictable.
They are dancing to a music I cannot hear. Finally I am leap-
ing in despair between them, as if between ice floes, for a few
million years without being able to reach land.

When I have almost got used to living in geological time,
short time comes back again, suddenly, like the handle when
you step on a rake.

9

Morning urine is thick and sluggish, highly concentrated; dark.
Faeces consist of small hard kernels like sheep droppings. I
drive out of Tan-Tan between drifts of sand like the heaps of
snow in Stockholm at winter and think: sand never melts.

I find it difficult to shake off the geological perspective of my dream. The landscape of the desert has no protective covering – the desert is geology exposed.

One of the few books Darwin had with him on his voyage on the *Beagle* was Charles Lyell's *Principles of Geology*. As he read it, he slowly realized that the earth was much older than he had thought. Not four thousand years but perhaps four thousand *million* years.

Time was given a depth it had never had before. What did Lyell feel, what did Darwin feel, looking down into those depths?

10

The first forty-one hundred million years of the history of the Sahara are still practically unknown today. All we know is that Africa then, as now, was a primaeval mountain plateau of granite.

Our earliest knowledge of the Sahara comes from a period when sedimentary types of rock had just begun to form layers on top of the primary rock. Africa then stood on its head roughly where the Antarctic now lies and the Sahara was covered with kilometre-thick inland ice. The ice left scrape-marks behind in Ordovician sandstone, marks found and interpreted five hundred million years later, in the 1970s.

The continent turned over as it slowly wandered northwards and for a while North Africa bordered on North America. Had the weather been more suitable, it would have been possible to walk dry-shod from Boston to Casablanca.

When the continents were wrenched free of each other, bits of Africa went with America and became eastern Massachusetts and one bit of Pennsylvania stayed behind in the western Sahara.

Four hundred million years ago, the Sahara was under water. Large parts of the oil deposits were formed in the sediment from that period. Three hundred and fifty million years ago, the climate turned warmer and the sea water retreated. Over two hundred million years, the Sahara was alternately land and sea. The last Saharan sea disappeared ten million years ago.

Eight million years ago, the Sahara was an even bigger desert than it is today. The Mediterranean was closed off from its connection with the Atlantic and after a thousand years it had dried out into a desert which lasted for several million years. Salt deposits from the evaporated water still lie on the seabed, found in 1960 and investigated by deep drilling in 1970.

Seventy thousand years ago, the Sahara began to turn green again, with trees and grass. But the same cold snap that made the temperature mild and pleasant in the Sahara turned Central Europe into a treeless tundra and covered North Europe with inland ice for over fifty thousand years.

Twelve thousand years ago, when the inland ice had retreated from Sweden, the Sahara was still green. But about six thousand years BC, a dry spell began and lasted for fifteen hundred years. Then the rains came back for a thousand years. A new dry period occurred between 3300 and 2500 BC. The next rainy period was short – only five hundred years. The present dry period began in about 2000 BC, so has lasted for four thousand years.

Very small changes in the world's average temperature –

only a degree or two – create an ice age in North America or a desert in the Sahara. At this moment, as I arrive, it is one of the hottest periods over the last million years. From a geological point of view, the apparent eternity of the Saharan desert is merely an episode between two European ice ages.

11

Where the road comes down to the sea there is a small fishing harbour, with screaming gulls swarming around it. The white foaming breakers roll in against sedimentary rock resembling clumps of plasticine. Along the edge of the plateau, often ten or so metres above the surface of the sea, lone fishermen walk with their long fishing rods. Poverty-stricken gatherers of brushwood and roots search for fuel for the night's fire.

People on this coast made their first contact with Europe when the Portuguese Henrique el Navegador sailed past in 1441. His men went ashore and captured twelve nomads to take with them.

Thus the manhunt began. The small fishing villages along the coast had nothing but stones and spears with which to defend themselves. In 1443, Eannes de Azurara relates:

Some were drowned in the sea, others hid in their cabins, yet others tried to bury their children in the sand in order to return later to fetch them. But Our Lord God, who rewards everything well done, decided as compensation for the hard work our men had done in His service that day to allow them to conquer their enemies and take 165 prisoners, men, women and children, not counting those killed or who killed themselves.

At the end of the 1400s, when Portugal and Spain divided up the world between them, the Spaniards were given the Saharan coast, as it lay close to the Spanish Canary Isles. But by the time four hundred Spaniards stepped ashore to take possession of the area, the Saharans had had time to organize resistance. Only a hundred Spaniards escaped with their lives. The hunt for slaves continued all through the 1500s, but for almost four hundred years the Saharans managed to prevent Europeans from gaining a foothold on the coast.

12

At the tip of the Cap Juby headland there is no archipelago, only one small island.

A Scot called Donald MacKenzie opened a store there in 1875. He called it the North West Africa Company and successfully traded cloth, tea and sugar for wool, leather and ostrich feathers.

The Sultan of Morocco disliked the competition. In 1895, he bought the store for £50,000 and closed it.

MacKenzie was also a thorn in the flesh of the Spanish traders on the Canary Isles, where he had a base. They wanted to take over his profitable caravan trade and exploit the rich coastal fishing grounds. In 1884, they sent men to the Sahara

Cap Juby from the air. (*Musée d'Air France*)

and built a fort on the next headland, the Dakla Peninsula, and called it Villa Cisneros.

The Saharans attacked the fort constantly, the caravans never turned up, profits were non-existent and the Spanish state had to take over.

By 1914, the French had subjugated the interior of the Sahara. In the north, they had occupied Morocco. In Europe, the First World War was being fought. Only in the Spanish Sahara was nothing happening. The commanding officer in Villa Cisneros, Fransisco Bens, had been rotting away there for ten years. Now he put his soldiers onto a ship and sailed north to capture Cap Juby.

The Admiralty found out and ordered the ship to return to Villa Cisneros immediately.

But Bens didn't give up. On foot, he marched his men north along the coast.

As they approached Cap Juby, they were overtaken by a Spanish cruiser, ordered to board and were once again conveyed ignominiously back to Villa Cisneros.

Not until 1916 was Bens finally able to occupy Cap Juby, this time at the request of the Saharans, who preferred Bens to the aggressive French, and also of the French, who preferred Bens to the aggressive Saharans.

Of course, by then trade had long gone elsewhere and MacKenzie's island became the Spanish equivalent of Devil's Island, a prison as loathed by the gaolers as it was feared by the prisoners.

Its little fort was surrounded by two kilometres of barbed wire, says Joseph Ressel, the French writer, there on a visit. At night, nowhere was safe outside the walls. It was difficult to tell the difference between soldiers and convicts: all were unshaven, unwashed and in the same ragged uniforms. The officers sat silently in the mess, playing dice, their faces expressionless.

But in the early 1920s, this godforsaken place gained a sudden importance when the French airline Compagnie Latécoère needed it as a stopover on the first Toulouse-Dakar air route.

And in the mid-1920s, when the Germans and the French were competing for the air routes to South America and German agents supplied the Saharans with arms and ammunition to shoot down French planes – then Cap Juby became a focal point.

In the spring of 1927, a new airport chief was appointed to Cap Juby with the task of rescuing shot-down French pilots and creating better relations with the Saharans. His name was Antoine de Saint-Exupéry.

13

I loved the airmen in Saint-Exupéry's books. The pilots of those days were kind of canoeists of the air, with no more than their lower bodies inside the 'flying machine', as it was called. Flying was shooting the rapids with the propellor as a paddle.

The primitive, single-engined machines flew below the clouds to see their way. In fog or a sandstorm, they were lost. One in six flights between Cap Juby and Dakar ended in a crash or emergency landing in the desert.

And when the pilot in his thick leather overalls, 'heavy and cumbersome as a diver', clambered out of his cockpit – then, if the rescuers did not get to him in time, what awaited him was captivity or death at the hands of hostile nomads. Altogether, 121 pilots were lost.

There was no shortage of exciting adventures in the boys' books of my childhood. But they had one failing – they had no idea what they were talking about.

If you asked Edward S. Ellis how Deerfoot behaved when he 'crept invisibly through the thicket', there would have been a silence. Ellis was not an Indian. He had no idea how it happened. I could see that already from the way he wrote.

Saint-Ex, on the other hand, was a real airman. He knew that the pilot can feel from the vibrations in his own body when fifteen tons of matter has achieved the 'maturity' required to take off. He knew what it felt like to separate the plane from the ground – 'with a movement like picking a flower' – and let it be borne by the air.

His knowledge was no thin veneer concealing massive

ignorance. He was authentic. When he called the desert sun 'a pale soap bubble in the mist', I knew he had seen it. He had been there. It was in his language.

Saint-Ex was the first writer who gave me some sense of what 'style' is.

14

Today, Cap Juby is called Tarfaya. I book in at the Green March hotel. There is no other.

The town is white with blue front doors and flat roofs, a forest of reinforcement rods protruding from the walls – the houses are all prepared for a second floor which has not yet arrived.

The small shops are just holes in the walls, all with an identical assortment of candies, cigarettes, batteries, sewing thread and soft drinks.

I start asking after old people who might have memories of the 1920s. Yes, there should be a few. But while I am waiting for them, a courteous Moroccan policeman comes and asks me to accompany him to the police station.

They already know everything there. The squealing radio with its crackling voices has told them where I have come from, where I have spent the night, which police posts I have passed, all my father's first names, all my mother's first names and her maiden name, and also that claim not to know the names of my father's father or my maternal grandmother.

So I want to talk to old Saharans in Tarfaya, do I? The

chief gendarme is full of goodwill. Tomorrow I am to meet the mayor. He will help me.

I am allowed to see the charming and obliging side of the system of control. Other people get the disappearances and the torture.

15

The front door of the Green March hotel is kept shut with a thick piece of paper folded twice and jammed in between the door and the doorpost. Whenever anyone fails to do this, the door swings open and slams violently in the wind.

There is a café on the ground floor. For dinner, I am served two eggs apparently fried in waste engine oil. I eat the bread with gratitude.

The café has the town's only television set. The news begins with the usual good wishes and other courtesies which Hassan, the King, has exchanged with other heads of state. Then comes what Hassan has done during the day, often with flashbacks to what Hassan had done previously on the same day or in the same genre. It ends with a prediction of what Hassan will do tomorrow, illustrated with film of what it looked like when Hassan last did the same thing.

The few seconds left at the end are devoted to other world news.

Then the screen goes blank. Everyone waits patiently. The landlord gets up, climbs onto a chair and puts in a video.

After ten minutes, the tape breaks. Everyone goes on calmly watching. The landlord runs the tape back and starts it again, the volume higher this time – rather like trying to get through a sandy stretch of road by backing the car, revving the engine and trying it faster.

But it's no use. The tape gives up at exactly the same place in the action.

No one moves a muscle. Everyone stays seated, full of confidence. The landlord goes to fetch another video. This time we go straight into the middle of a quite different story, the beginning missing. No one reacts. Everyone gratefully goes on watching.

All night the door slams violently in the wind blowing off the sea.

16

A man has gasped all his life, then draws his first really deep breath. After 'a life of gasping', as he calls it, he at last, slowly, with great enjoyment, drinks a large glass of cold air.

17

A tall yellow building behind the main street dominates the town. The walls are crowned with watchtowers, with open fields of fire in all directions. This is where Colonel Bens resided in 1925. Now it is the Moroccan mayor's office.

The mayor sits below a preternaturally large photograph of

Hassan and wears an Italian 'camel-hair ulster' made of nylon. With him are some old people in real, smelly camel-hair clothes, among them the son of the interpreter who accompanied Saint-Ex on his flights.

He tells me about an emergency landing in the desert. His father kept the 'bandits' at a distance with his rifle while Saint-Ex repaired the engine. They took off at dusk with bullets whistling round their ears.

'That man saved my life,' said Saint-Ex. Afterwards it was all made into a film so that the whole world could see it.

'Were you there yourself?'

'Not me. But Ahmed was.'

The mayor promises to summon Ahmed the next day.

18

I know which tiles are loose on the steep hotel stairs. Even in the darkness, I can find the footrest of the squatting-toilet. Life in Tarfaya is becoming familiar.

In the mornings, I breakfast on bread and water. Decades old, the bed I am sitting on still has the plastic covering it had been transported in. That probably increases its second-hand value. The bottom sheet is the kind that only goes as far as your knees. There is no top sheet.

Through the little window I can see across the constantly windswept headland to the island with its dark, abandoned prison. Some boys are playing football on the shore, in the wind coming off the sea.

The mayor's office opens at eight-thirty, but there is no

point going there until half-past ten. I sit in the sun outside the hotel and warm up as I wait. The greengrocer puts his wooden boxes out on the pavement. You buy bread from a blue hatch. A Saharan in a white jibba walks past. They are a rare sight here. Uniformed Moroccans are in the majority.

A small girl with a school bag buys some carrots. A man walks past with a large bunch of fragrant mint. His feet are cracked. Fish are being weighed on the corner – some a type of perch, vertically striped or long and silvery with horizontal stripes, glittering in the morning light.

At about half-past ten, I meet Ahmed, aged eighty-five.

'Saint-Ex was different. He tried to learn our language. None of the Spaniards did that. He studied with a teacher of the Koran called Sidi l'Hussein Oueld n'Ouesa. The Spaniards just sat in their fort. They didn't fly. But Saint-Ex was a travelling man, so he had to be able to speak languages. He was a man who knew how to negotiate and often did so over men held for ransom.'

'Is it true that the tribes shot at the French planes?'

'Of course.' He smiles inwardly as though lost in happy memories.

'Why?'

This causes a certain confusion. Naturally they shot, but why?

Gradually the intellectual explanation appears: we were defending ourselves against colonialism. Then comes the current opportune explanation: we were acting on the orders of the Sultan of Morocco. Anyhow, they lived off taking prisoners and demanding ransoms. Why then shouldn't they shoot?

The Moor doesn't defend his freedom, for in the desert
you are always free. No visible treasures, for the desert is
bare. No, the Moor defends a secret realm and that's
why I admire him.

The aristocrat Saint-Ex has a tendency to ennoble everything
that arouses his admiration.

He ennobles the airline pilots as a new aristocracy of the air.
He ennobles their opponents, 'the Moor', as knights of an
exotic realm of pride.

He romanticizes the bearers of a new and unknown technology and a distant unknown people – and so defends old
familiar feudal values, rejected by capitalist Europe.

Saint-Ex could not have known about the invisible treasures
the desert does in fact contain, for phosphates, iron ore and oil
had still not been found in the Sahara. But that it was their
freedom the Saharans were defending – he ought to have
known that.

He had done his military service in conquered Morocco. He
had travelled in conquered Algeria. He knew that freedom is not
something the desert automatically provides. 'The Moors' on the
African Atlantic coast in 1927 were in fact the last unsubjugated
Saharans – a result of the outstanding weakness of the Spanish
colonial powers and the Moors' own bitter resistance.

Perhaps it was natural that Saint-Ex could not support this
struggle for freedom, as it was at him and his friends the
Saharans were shooting with their German Mauser rifles.

But he never even realized what the struggle was about. It
all became romanticism.

20

White garden furniture dazzles my eyes. I recognize it from previous dreams. Why does it keep coming back? The table and chairs are not spray-lacquered, but their wide boards are painted with layer after layer of thick oil paint. They are not 'creamy white', for there is no tinge of yellow, but the colour has the fat puffiness of whipped cream. The light is reflected from the gleaming white surfaces with a force that makes my eyes smart and everyone squint. Which everyone? Don't know. Their faces are empty, obliterated, wiped out like my whole childhood.

There is no one to ask. They are all dead. But from the depths of the past, this table throws out a sunspot strong enough to wake me up.

21

The next morning while I sit warming up outside the hotel, the garbage cart comes past, drawn by a mule. The garbage pails are emptied into the open cart, just as used to happen in Älvsjö when I was a child. On the corner they are selling yellow dates on stems, gathered in bunches like the birch sprigs and coloured feathers of Lent at home.

Today's old man points out the exact place where the Frenchman's house stood: right next to the fortress wall on the side facing the airfield. They used to hear music from there at night, notes from an old gramophone he wound up by hand.

For company he had four animals: cat, dog, a chimpanzee and a hyena.

In the evenings I carefully transfer this information from my tape recorder into my notebook. I think I can at last see Saint-Ex fairly clearly in front of me as he sits at his desk, surrounded by his animals.

The light flows from the lamp like oil. I see him dipping his pen into the inkwell, which I used to do when I was learning to write. The sea roars out there in the darkness, the cries of the guards on duty echoing between the walls. A light rain appears to be falling – the sound of the moist night air condensing on the metal roof. Sand crunches between the papers on the desk. Saint-Ex is writing.

When he leaves Cap Juby eighteen months later, he has with him the manuscript of his first novel, *Southern Mail*. And within him he is carrying what are the as-yet-unwritten desert stories in *The Little Prince* and *Wind, Sand and Stars*.

22

What fascinated me as a boy when I read those books was their belief that the airman was a new kind of man.

A person taking off from the ground also elevated himself above the trivialities of life into a new understanding, created by the particular experiences modern technology made possible.

The airman was not yet a captain in the routine trade between tax-free shops of the world's cities. Like the astronaut now, the airman was the most modern man of his day, a

Saint-Exupéry and his best friend, Henri Guillaumet, standing in front of their plane. (*Musée d'Air France*)

representative of the future on a temporary stopover in what was soon to be the past.

That gave him tremendous authority, which Saint-Ex used to ask yet again the great questions.

What is man? What are we for?

Man makes himself, he said.

We aren't born man, we become that.

We become that through solidarity with each other.

We become that by taking responsibility.

I loved his gravity when he said such things, quite shamelessly, with the same endless trust in his reader as the airman had in the empty air. In that solemnity, he was so close to me, I could lean forward and touch him.

He taught me to demand of a writer not just excitement and adventure, but also knowledge, seriousness and presence. Presence most of all.

If the writer is not there himself in his writing, how can he demand that you should be?

To Smara

23

'Like a pearl-diver, I must immediately return,' wrote Michel Vieuchange in his diary.

Michel read *Southern Mail* when it was published in 1928. He was four years younger than Saint-Ex. He had also read Nietzsche and Rimbaud, and had done his military service in Morocco, and he, too, had dreams of the desert. One September day in 1930, disguised as a woman, he disappeared into the unsubjugated tribal area some miles north of Tiznit. He was on his way to Smara.

Saint-Ex never got that far.

But every morning he did fly one of the off-duty Cap Juby planes to drive the condensation out of the cylinders – planes at that time had to be rested like horses – and sometimes he diverged from the flight path along the coast. Once he flew right into 'the mysterious Smara with its virginal ruins, as forbidden to the white man as Timbuctoo'.

In actual fact, Timbuctoo had been occupied by the French in 1893, and Smara was no more forbidden than that. It was destroyed by French troops in 1913. But the ruins were still defended by the Saharan tribes. Just flying over Smara was a bold, almost foolish act.

Vieuchange was now heading that way. On foot.

24

I go by car.

It is a peculiar day. All week the wind has blown in off the sea but now it is coming from the desert, hot as a hairdryer. The runway in Tarfaya has been shrouded in wet sea mist; today it is shrouded in the hot dry haze of pure dust.

I scrape the sand off the car just as one scrapes snow off a car in a Swedish winter, and as I drive into the white haze it is like driving into a snowstorm. Only slowly does it occur to me that because I am in the desert, this must be a sandstorm.

Twilight descends in the early morning and my field of vision shrinks so that I can see only a few metres ahead. When I stop and get out of the car, I find it difficult to keep my balance. The sand stabs like icy pins at my unprotected face. It is impossible to breathe into the wind. I hurry back into the car and drive on as fast as I dare through the mounting drifts.

The sand is not slippery, but occasionally it is treacherously loose, and sometimes as hard-packed as stone. The dust is finer than snow and penetrates the car so that the air is thick to breathe. The smell is sharply mineral, quite unlike the euphoric fragrance of snow.

Most of all, the physical feeling is different. The body suffocates when it sweats without sweat. Moisture vanishes immediately off the skin, leaving a crackled layer of salt which encloses the body as if in a mould.

When I was small, I often fantasized about sandstorms. Before falling asleep, I surrounded myself with the whistling, biting haze. To be able to breathe, I walked backwards, into the wind. My watch filled with sand and stopped. I drank the last drops from my crumpled water-holder and knew I had to die.

In these sandstorm dreams, there was always a mirror-like lake of clear fresh water which saved my life just before I slipped into sleep.

To believe in water in the desert is not as crazy as it seems. Sometimes it actually rains. At this moment my childish dreams come true, the dreams of desert pools glimmering in hollows and a green veil thrown over the sand. I drive through a green desert gleaming with moisture – although the whole of the Sahara is heading towards me and I am almost suffocated.

No traffic comes towards me. At a turn-off to Boucraa, I am stopped by a military column: open vehicles, dark snow-goggles, on full alert. The Polisario, the Saharan liberation movement, usually strike in the shelter of a sandstorm.

I turn back and spend the night in El Aaiun. Two tank battles are fought that night, one near Boucraa, between Moroccan troops and the still-unconquered Saharans.

Vieuchange tried to get to Smara disguised as a woman. His posthumous journal shows him preoccupied with the actual disguise and the conditions his female rôle forces him into.

He shaves his legs. He learns not to show his hands. He always lies curled up like a dog, never on his back – only a Jewess lies on her back. He sits with his knees wide apart, never close together. When he rides, he keeps his heels lower than his toes.

In daytime, he is bathed in sweat inside the blue garment which envelops him like a tent. He longs in vain to feel the wind

Michel Vieuchange, dressed as a Berber woman.

on his face, to be able to move freely. He wants to know where he is. He wants to see the great expanses of desert. He wants to see the men coming and going. But all he sees is the ground.

Few accounts of the Sahara deal so much with the actual ground in the desert, the small broken stones, the gravel, the stony riverbeds, the dark tormented soil. That is all he sees.

He doesn't see the sunrise, only a golden wave of light sweeping over the ground, leaving behind it small lakes of night in the hollows.

In the towns, he sees nothing but the room in which he is imprisoned like a criminal: the rough walls that crumble at his touch, the low sooty ceiling and the light let in by deep holes so narrow he can't see out.

In the heat, he pours water over his veiled head so the evaporation will provide him with a little cool. The meat hanging from the ceiling is invisible beneath its carpet of flies. He doesn't eat any of it. He hardly eats anything at all, but lives off sweet mint tea.

On cold damp nights, the women press their bodies against his to seek warmth – or perhaps with other intentions which simply fill him with distaste. Frozen and soaked through, he waits for the golden wave of sunrise finally to sweep over the ground, this ground which is all he sees.

26

I am living in a stable together with a naked gnarled old woman with long breasts hanging down below her waist. She is kind to me. It's only her horse that's pigheaded.

She has the horse up in a hayloft with the railing missing. Nothing but its own instinct for self-preservation keeps the horse from falling down.

When I come up to the hayloft, the horse eagerly starts nuzzling my hand and pockets for the sugar it is used to being given. I try to get down again, but the horse bars my way as it nuzzles through my clothes and my body more and more intimately and insistently. Not until the woman comes up and gives the horse some lumps of sugar can I leave.

It strikes me when I see her breasts that perhaps she is my mother and that it is my own greed, greater than the horse's, that has made them so long.

27

The sky is clear again the next morning. The sand-sweeper is already busy sweeping away the drifts. Every tuft has a small train of sand pointing away from the wind.

A few miles outside El Aaiun, a gang of Saudi falconers have their caravan camp. They hunt for partridges over great distances with the aid of sophisticated radar equipment, pursuing them in four-wheel-drive vehicles, then, taking the hood off the specially trained falcons, for a few exhilarating moments experience their own power as the falcon cruises above its prey, strikes, kills and brings back the meat.

'The price per kilo will have been considerable,' say my Saharan hitchhikers dryly.

They are elegant young men with knife-edge creases in their trousers and smart briefcases. At their destination some miles further on, I go with them to two tents by the roadside. The tents smell of milk. Some women live an outfield life there with their goats.

They splash us with lavender water from a litre bottle and call out to the retired soldier in the tent next to them. My hitchhikers and the old man begin the usual ping-pong game of courtesies and mutual exchanges of information. The smart town lads are transformed into scions of herdsmen, and with surprising expertise they carry out the traditional tea ceremony.

'If you were staying any longer, I would have slit the throat of a goat for you,' says the old man.

He is lying on a plaited mat, kneading a large cushion on his stomach. The air is fresh and pleasant under the sky-blue tent, the roof shutting off the sun but giving free rein to the wind. The charcoal glowing in the chafing dish ticks metallically and there is a strong smell of mint and goat's milk.

After the obligatory three cups, I drive on towards Smara through vast flat countryside, punctuated by odd tussocks and groups of heroic tamarisks.

Right out in the dryness, I again meet a large cloud of grasshoppers coming from the south-east, not so much flying as being blown my way by the desert wind, bowling along the ground like a gigantic wavering wheel of insects, some young and pink-winged, but most mature, well-filled, golden-winged creatures which strike the car with a crashing sound and are crushed.

The Hotel Goldsand, the best in Smara, has been requisitioned by the governor. At the Hotel Erraha across the street, I am given the only room with a window. Two beds, and a hook in the wall. A handbasin outside the privy at the end of the corridor. A pound a night.

I go to bathe after the dusty journey. On my way I see a notice: *Club Saquia el Hamra Musculation.* Bodybuilding in the Sahara! Suddenly I feel my muscles aching with a longing for exertion.

The premises have just opened for the day and are still empty. I hang my clothes on the wall and start warming up.

As I lie in the leg-press, an intellectual Moroccan wearing glasses comes and shows me how I can get greater play by pulling out a peg. He is a bookkeeper in the civilian administration and has been here for three years, his family in Casa, as they call Casablanca. Goes home to see them every third month.

We train together and alternate three times fifteen with light weights. There is – he says, in the winter as well, but most of all in the summer when Smara is turned into a reeking hell – there is a yawning chasm between official rhetoric and the reality of war-weariness and longing for home. The Sahara has been designated 'their' country, but it certainly is not their climate or their landscape when they come from northern Morocco . . .

After the long gap in my training, it is wonderful to feel my muscles working again, at first reluctantly, then more and more delighted at being needed. The ego-experience climbs down from my head and out into my limbs. Bit by bit my body comes back and becomes my own again.

After training, we go on to the bath-house. In the innermost of the steaming rooms, we mix hot water from one tap with cold water from another into our black rubber buckets and spend the rest of the afternoon scooping, soaping and scrubbing our newly found bodies while listening to the splash of water against tiles and the murmur of voices under the vaulted ceiling.

There is no wind in there. The light doesn't hurt your eyes. Your nails don't split. You don't get sand in your mouth. The air is not prickly dry in your nose. On the contrary, it is thick with steaming moisture and feels soft and smooth in the hollows of your body. Good water flows. In the desert, that is paradise.

29

The human body has six hundred muscles. You use most of them automatically without experiencing them. The best part of training is finding new muscles which have never been conscious before.

How many muscles has a human life? You're sure to use most of them automatically, without experiencing them. Particularly in long-term relationships, developing a routine is labour saving, and thus enervating. The best part of suddenly encountering solitude is that it provides training: you discover your life when you have to start using its long-since forgotten and atrophied muscles.

30

I am living on a hillside, the road meandering past. I wake early and go out for a newspaper.

The news on the front page is criss-crossed with thick black lines which make them invalid and partly illegible. There is only one legible and valid item of news. That is printed in microscopic typescript and says that the country has been invaded by a foreign power. The foreign troops can be expected at any moment to pass along this particular road.

Then I suddenly remember that I had a goat as well as a dog when I left. But the dog is too faithful and the goat too rebellious and unmanageable. So I have tied them up in the forest. I was thinking of fetching them later, but forgot them. Are they still alive? Has anyone found them? Have they died of starvation? I must find out before the foreigners get here. But how shall I get there? My wife is already messing about in the garden. The children will soon wake up. So far, I am the only one who knows about the invasion, about the goat, about the dog – and what shall I do?

I go and ask my father. He has put a piece of white paper in front of him on his desk. He takes out his pocket-knife with its mother-of-pearl inlays, slots a nail into the groove and opens the knife. It is the small sharp blade he opens out. Without a word he starts slowly and carefully cutting away the white on his nails.

He isn't cutting his nails. He is trimming them. He prunes them, just as you prune a tree or a bush in the garden. He cuts off just that part of the nail which helped him open the knife.

I say nothing. Father is also silent. With a scraping sound, the slice of nail falls onto the white paper.

31

The first inhabitants of Smara were black and came from the south. Their rock engravings show a Saharan savanna where elephants and giraffes grazed.

In the millennium before our era, they were driven back south by the drought. Those who stayed behind were subjugated by Berber peoples from the north, who rode horses and had weapons made of iron.

The desert deepened all around them. The horse was followed by the camel, which arrived from the east around the year 100 and made possible the regular caravan trade across the desert.

In the year 1000, there was a gang of Saharans who called themselves the 'Almoravids'. They took over the caravan trade, penetrated northwards and conquered Morocco and Spain. There we got to know them by the name of *Moors*.

In the thirteenth century, all the Saharans who stayed behind in the desert were conquered by a Bedouin tribe, Beni Hassan, emigrating from Yemen. Hassanic Arabic pushed out the Berber language, Znaga. The ruling Arabs accepted tributes from their Znaga vassals who in turn ruled over the black indigenous population: slaves and freed slaves. A council, *djema*, drew up laws and chose a chieftain.

The most famous of these chieftains was Ma Ainin, 'The Water of the Eyes'. He founded Smara in 1895 as the centre for the Saharan tribes and his headquarters in the struggle against the Europeans.

The main enemy was the French, pressing from the south through Mauritania, from the east through Algeria and soon enough from the north through Morocco. That was why

Vieuchange had to travel in disguise. He belonged to the enemy.

Smara was not colonized until 1934 when the Spaniards, with the help of the French, occupied the town.

Decolonization also came late. The Spaniards were not prepared to hand over power to the Polisario until the mid-1970s.

But the King of Morocco had territorial ambitions. He dreamt of a Greater Morocco that would include parts of Algeria, Mali and Mauritania, and on down to the Senegal river. He maintained that Spanish West Sahara belonged to him for historic reasons.

The matter was referred to the international court at the Hague, which replied that there were indeed legal ties between Morocco and West Sahara, but that these ties did not entail territorial supremacy. The principle of the right to self-determination through the free declaration of the will of the people should, the court decided, be applied without restriction.

32

What happened next was extremely peculiar. Only in Smara has anything like it ever happened to me.

One evening, I am sitting in the corridor of the Hotel Erraha, talking to a Moroccan greengrocer. He is from Rabat and has been tempted to Smara with subsidies from the government. Here he has a cheap house, earns good money and likes it. And as evidence that there are no problems in the town, he alleges there are no soldiers there.

'No soldiers, no problems.'

He says this in the Hotel Erraha, which is full of soldiers on leave.

They are sleeping in heaps on the floor of the corridor in front of us.

They have come directly from the fighting at the Wall erected as a defence against the Polisario, sand running off their uniforms, wild-eyed, heads wrapped in cloths and rags. With its music, its lights and occasional women, Smara to them is a paradise compared with the dry dust, the eternal wind and the shadeless heat out there.

Maybe they have no other problems, but they are undeniably soldiers.

Through the hotel window, the greengrocer and I look out over the town. It consists mainly of military installations resembling cartons of eggs with their rows of yellowish-white cupolas. Behind the hotel, army vehicles are lined up in a gigantic military parking lot. In the street below we can see military police walking around in pairs, checking Saharan identity cards. Moroccan conscripts roam in groups along the street, hanging onto each other like teenage girls. A column of army trucks – with their engines running – is ready to depart to the front. The trucks are full of soldiers with closed, sullen, bitter faces.

But the greengrocer maintains they don't exist.

'But hang on a minute,' I say, in appeal. 'You can't even go and have a pee without falling over sleeping soldiers. It's seething with them down there on the street . . .'

I point out through the window. But that makes no impression on the greengrocer.

'Further away maybe,' he says. 'But here in Smara there are no soldiers, no problems.'

Is he saying what the police have told him to say without bothering to make it plausible? Does he wish, while protecting himself, to tell me the exact opposite: 'Many soldiers, many problems'?

I don't know. All I know is that our conversation ceased once it lost touch with reality.

33

On October 16, 1975, when the international court decision was delivered, the Moroccan invasion of West Sahara was already planned in detail. Hassan II was unable to back down. He did the same thing as the greengrocer.

He made a great speech in Rabat, explaining that the international court had upheld Morocco's demands.

To objections that it had done no such thing, he simply declined to answer. Instead he announced a 'peace march' to 'liberate' West Sahara.

At this threat, the Spaniards suddenly broke off all contact with the Saharans. A curfew was proclaimed. The Spanish Foreign Legion erected barbed wire all around Saharan neighbourhoods. Saharan soldiers were dismissed from the army. Petrol stations stopped selling petrol to Saharans. In a week, twelve thousand Spanish civilians were flown out of the country. Even corpses were evacuated. A thousand dead were dug up out of the local cemeteries and flown to the Canary Isles. The animals in the zoo went with them.

The Spaniards persistently denied 'rumours' that they were going to hand over power to the King of Morocco. But in secret they had already done so.

By the time Moroccan troops marched in, the majority of

Smara's Saharan population had fled across the border into Algeria, 150 miles east. Smara, the main centre of the Saharan liberation movement, became the main base for King Hassan's war of conquest in the Sahara.

34

'Problems? In that case, it's the goats,' says the governor.

We are invited to dinner at the governor's palace. A roast sheep with its ribs exposed like a shipwreck is carried in as we sit there on the sofa, all men, all Moroccans, except me and a Saharan poet. Chicken with orange peel and olives comes next, then sweet rice with almonds, raisins and cinnamon completing the meal.

'The nomads make their way from the drought in to the water and electricity of the towns,' says the governor. 'They settle, motorized herdsmen tending their herds from Landrovers and keeping their families wherever there is a school for their children and healthcare for their old.

'It is worst for the women. They know nothing except about goats. The woman belongs with goats. Goats are closer to her than her husband, yes, even closer than her children. Her way of bringing up children is out of date, her cooking primitive, and only goats give her a *raison d'être*. So she can't live without goats. She takes them with her into town. The whole town is full of goats and that creates hygiene problems. It's simply impossible in modern apartments. I have no hesitation in saying that goats are the greatest social problem we have to contend with at the moment.'

'And the solution?'

'I have issued a goat order and appointed one person responsible for goats in each neighbourhood. He sees to it that the neighbourhood is kept free of goats. Each neighbourhood has also been allocated an area outside town, where the goats are allowed. It keeps the women busy – it's a long walk there to do the milking.'

35

The Saharan poet Yara Mahjoub is a handsome man of about fifty with brilliant white teeth and a skipper's wreath of short white hair. He can't write, not even his name. He carries the whole of his repertoire within him.

'Is it ten poems? Or a hundred?' I ask.

'Oh, many many more! I'd be able to recite them to you all night and all the next day and still have many unspoken.'

'What are they about?'

'Give me a subject and I shall sing the praises of it.'

I suggest 'the judgement of the international court' and he is immediately prepared.

> *Sahara reunited with the mother country*
> *the profound connection*
> *between Saharans and the throne –*
> *the evidence now in the hands of the Hague*
> *where it's been confirmed by the court*
> *so everyone must be convinced.*

He turns to the assembled company and recites the poem with great bravura, an artist used to performing. Every gesture is part of a stage language, every line in the verse demanding applause.

'When did you compose your first poem?'

'It was during the vaccination year, which is also called the "year of the summer rain". I was eighteen and in love for the first time. This is what it sounded like:

> *'Oh how beautiful it is,*
> *the bridge leading to the hill!*
> *Oh how lovely is the hill's blue*
> *in her eyes!'*

'That was in the days of the Spaniards. Did you compose poems in their honour?'

'I had my camel and my goats. I didn't need the Spaniards. Father was a goldsmith. So am I. That is my profession. Poetry is my vocation. If I don't make poems, I fall ill. All real poetry demands inspiration and the love of the King is the greatest source of inspiration. I made this poem during His visit to the USA:

> *'After your journey to the States*
> *and your visit to the Pentagon*
> *your insignificant neighbours scream,*
> *they who are a thorn in your side,*
> *they who rise against Your Majesty,*
> *they scream as if mad with envy.*
> *But they lack food,*
> *yea, they lack soap!'*

36

One night on his way to Smara, Michel Vieuchange hears far-distant men singing Saharan songs together in the darkness.

As he listens to the resolute gravity in their voices, he thinks there is something peculiar about his own enterprise. What is he really doing there? Is he going to do violence to a secret which ought to remain untouched?

Justified qualms. But he waves them away and struggles on, drunk with fatigue, exhausted, but upright. Elation pours through him despite his torments. He feels chosen, happy, purified by his own flame.

Sometimes his mouth is so dry he has great difficulty pronouncing the single word 'Ahmed'. He prepares himself for several minutes before attempting it. Only one single word and it seems almost insurmountable.

One of his Saharan companions falls ill and refuses to go on. The little caravan returns to Tiglit. Again Vieuchange is imprisoned in a room with no window, a cloud of flies his only company.

His head is full of one single desire, firm and irrevocable: to complete his journey. He will carry out what he has made up his mind to do. Everything that has been working its way within him since birth is heading towards that goal.

His determination is unyielding. But during the long days of waiting, it changes character.

The thought of Smara no longer gives him any joy. He can no longer find the enthusiasm that has previously borne him along. It has dried out, shrivelled up.

Vieuchange in Tiglit, after his first attempt on Smara.

Decisions are nearly always carried out under different conditions from those under which they are made.

Decisions are made at headquarters. They are carried out in the trenches.

Decisions are made in Paris. They are carried out in the Sahara.

The emotions generated in him by the name 'Smara' have disappeared. Remaining is the decision. The will. The intention. When all the humidity has gone, in the end there is nothing left but defiance.

When desire burns out, it is replaced with lies. Vieuchange begins to pretend.

He writes 'we' about himself. He pretends he is not alone but travelling with his brother.

He pretends they are on an important assignment through unknown country where no one else has ever seen what they see. In reality, he knows who has been there before him and he has no assignment other than to carry out his own intention.

He pretends they are on their way to a living town. In reality, he knows perfectly well Smara is in ruins and that it was his own countrymen who destroyed it.

These false premises make his enterprise utterly artificial. But this artificiality is documented with extreme authenticity.

Step by step, stone by stone, he describes what it means to do something in the Sahara because he 'had wanted it, in Paris'.

38

On November 1, he finally arrives in Smara. He has spent most of the journey hidden in a pannier, curled up in a foetal position, tormented by unbearable cramps, not even seeing the ground.

He now breaks free and staggers off into town.

The ground is strewn with dark stones. Not a human being in sight. Everything is in ruins.

He buries a bottle with a message in it to show that he and his brother have 'discovered' Smara – a final game of pretence before he crawls back into the pannier and begins the return journey.

Vieuchange in front of Smara.

'I got there,' he writes in his journal. 'But like a pearl-diver, I must immediately return.'

He spent three hours in Smara. The return journey took a month. He died in Agadir on November 30, 1930.

Actual cause of death: dysentery.

Real cause of death: romanticism.

To Laghouat

39

'The more light the desert receives, the darker it seems to become,' writes Eugène Fromentin.

Desert romanticism exists in that kind of paradox. Otherwise one must ask what a romantic is doing in the desert at all. The desert has no leafy groves, fragrant meadows, deep-soughing forests, or anything else which usually evokes in the romantic the right emotions. Desert romanticism already appears incomprehensible at a distance. Up close, it becomes absurd. What is romantic about an endless gravel pit?

Eugène Fromentin can tell you what. He wrote the classic desert book *A Summer in the Sahara* (1857). He is the first of a long line of writers and artists to experience the desert with an aesthetic eye.

Fromentin loves the desert because it has no appeal, because it is never lovely. He loves the expansiveness of its lines, the

Eugène Fromentin, *Arab Horseman.* (*Musée des Beaux-Arts de La Rochelle*)

Eugène Fromentin, *Interior of Arab tailor's workshop.*
(*Private collection, descendants of Eugène Fromentin*)

emptiness of its space, the barrenness of its ground. At last a
sea which does not swell, but consists of a firm, immovable
body. At last a silence which is never broken in a desolate
country where no one comes and no one goes.

Strangely, that same silence seems so threatening in the
town, lying there dark and mute under the sun.

The people appear to have lost their power of speech. They
surround him with an immeasurable gravity, as mute and
scorched as the landscape they inhabit.

Why this silence? Is it the sun? The heat makes the air vibrate
with a faint but entirely audible note. The ground itself seems to
gasp. Day and night change places. The midday sun annihilates
and kills, the midnight darkness revives and gives life.

Fromentin sets off on nightly wanderings in town. But the
inhabitants are just as hostile in the dark hours. They do not
greet him. They pretend not to see him.

So that is what the Arab is – a man unwilling to show you his house, unwilling to say his name or say what he is doing or tell you where he is going. 'All curiosity is unwelcome to him.'

It must be the sun which has made the Arab like that. Fromentin feels himself being influenced. The sun persecutes him right into the night. 'I dream light,' he complains.

He stands all day out in the desert, painting, bathing in the sun. In the evening he is feverish from all the light his body has absorbed. Even when he closes his eyes he sees sparks, flames and circles of light in the darkness. 'I have no night, so to speak.'

People of the desert have lived under that sun since they were children. The terrible desert sun has marked them with its lack of emotion 'which has fallen from the sky onto objects and from objects has transferred to their faces'.

Hence the silence.

40

I've come from Algiers. I have rented a small Renault 4, buckled at all four corners and with the driver's seat sagging so much that it hits the floor. They did not want to let any other car go out into the desert. 'A single sandstorm takes off the paintwork in a few hours,' they said. So I put a couple of books and a rolled-up towel behind me and steered the little wreck out into the traffic of Algiers.

Algiers is a climbing town, all the streets on their way upwards or downwards, the traffic heavy and eternally at a standstill, until it suddenly hurtles forward with the roar of a tiger. I have seldom come across such a constant need to demonstrate the potency of your automobile and your driver's daring as I have here.

In a R4, there is nothing to do but calmly allow yourself to be passed on both sides, often so closely that your crumpled shirt gets a pressing into the bargain. So I cope with the latest passer's stinking exhaust fumes, perhaps muttering something about the fact that he is driving on camel shit to honour his mother.

Arabic oaths are often descriptions of the sexual behaviour with camels of the mother of the person concerned. Anyone who manages to combine the anal insult with the sexual gains extra points.

The road slices up the mountainside in sharp turns like a fretsaw. The R4 has no strength to fall back on – the trick is to accelerate between gears, as in the old days of double-declutching, and keep the engine running. Then the tough little car manages the Atlas mountains, and when I finally reach level ground, we get up to 60 mph, even 70 in successful moments.

It rumbles and it sways, but I can't help liking the R4 for the wind whistling through the coachwork and the sewing-machine buzz of the engine as it patiently carries me towards Laghouat.

Algeria is in the middle class of the world's countries. That is clear from the road, which is not dominated by shepherds and flocks of sheep but by heavy transporters – steel girders, pipes, cement. Roadworks occupy more machines than people – though the unemployed, currently 17%, would fight to be allowed to shovel macadam.

In the villages I try to buy some food for lunch, but there is only bread. There is always bread, subsidized by billions, very cheap to buy and sold in great quantities. Fresh morning bread has already been thrown away at midday to be replaced by even fresher afternoon bread. Even far out in the countryside, these bread habits have been adopted from the French and are considered sacred – Algeria literally throws away her oil income in the form of dry bread. A country which on liberation in 1962 was a great exporter of food now produces only 35% of what its people eat or throw away.

'*C'est la crise, c'est normale*,' they say in the shops as an explanation for there being no tea, no coffee, no sugar, no eggs – well, more or less nothing but detergents and powdered milk.

But there are schools. Everywhere I see children on their way to or from school. The first shift begins at dawn, the last is on its way home as the sun sets. Caring for the children and giving them an education despite 3.2% annual growth in population is the heroic feat of the schoolteachers – minor intellectuals who for twenty-five years have accepted these triple shifts, these remote posts in the countryside and these low salaries, to cope with the great task of teaching the people to read. But who feel themselves more and more deceived and abandoned as the years go by and others enrich themselves.

What did their sacrifices give them? When will things get better? In twenty years, when the oil runs out?

I stay with a teacher's family in Laghouat. My friend Ali, whom I got to know in the rue Valetin gym in Algiers. His brother Ahmed is leader of the big band 'Desert Brothers'. Like most young Algerians, they are enraged by the corrupt misrule.

'Before independence, we had five parties in the country. Now we're not considered mature enough to have more than one. What people lack is not maturity, but power!'

All evening we sit round the big couscous dish until the

meal is concluded with milk and dates. Then we all sleep together in the best room.

The moisture from our breathing glistens on the cold walls. Outside, the stars sparkle as brightly as only desert and darkness can make them. The silence is boundless, and the occasional distant barking of a dog makes it audible.

41

Early in the morning, I go up onto the roof. It is a beautiful day. White clouds have accumulated on the horizon like a further layer of sediment on dark mountains.

This is where Fromentin stood 130 years ago. The landscape we see is the same. The same sun, the same desert.

But not the same people. His Arabs were closed, menacing, hostile. Those I have met are open, lively, hospitable people.

Under the same sun.

Fromentin was wrong to think the merciless sun had marked the people of the desert for ever. Perhaps he actually knew that himself. In the 1980s, *A Summer in the Sahara* was published in new academic editions which also account for variations in the text. In them you find other explanations for the silence in Laghouat.

42

In the spring of 1830, Paris was already seething with the rebellion which was to find its outlet in the July revolution. De Polignac's militantly reactionary government was about to fall. As a final way of diverting dissatisfaction, it was decided to attack Algiers, on the pretext of an alleged insult to the French Consul.

In their proclamations to the people, the French said they had come to liberate the Arabs from Turkish oppression and make them 'lords in their own mansions'. But the supposed liberators committed the most hideous atrocities and retained power wherever they could seize it.

France under the July monarchy decided to keep just Algiers and its immediate surroundings; but the military was not to be deterred. Villages were burnt down in their hundreds, and thousands of refugees died of starvation. By the time the February revolution introduced the second empire, Algerian resistance had been broken all along the coast.

The mountains and the deserts remained. No political decision could stop the conquest that continued with military logic. On December 3, 1852, it was Laghouat's turn. The French seized the town after a two-day siege. Forty-five years later, the commanding officer described in his memoirs what happened next:

The town had to endure all the horrors of war, experience all the atrocities that can be committed by soldiers when they are left for a moment to themselves, still feverish from the dreadful fighting, raging over the dangers they have undergone and the losses they have suffered, excited by their hard-won victory. Terrible scenes were enacted.

Fromentin arrived in the early summer of 1853, scarcely six months after the massacre. 'I feel neither joy nor happiness here,' he writes. 'Difficult to explain why . . .'

43

Every morning, I go up onto the roof and sit there for a while, looking out over the brown slopes surrounding the town. They are covered with fresh green bushes and trees, although everywhere the actual ground is dry and infertile. The moisture has retreated from the sun and the winds, further down into the ground. That is where the roots seek it out.

Yesterday I drove through flowering nerium, a bush named after the Greek word for water, *nero*. It has a brilliant ability to find water at great depths and human water-diviners have always followed its roots.

The contrast between surface and depths, between what the eye sees up here and the real circumstances down there, are the fundamental experience of the desert.

From my viewpoint on the roof, I can follow the route of the victorious French into town. Fromentin did the same when the stench of corpses was still in the air. A French lieutenant who was present told him:

We literally waded in blood, and for two days it was impossible to get anywhere for the heaps of corpses.

Not only hundreds of men, shot or with bayonet wounds all over them, but also – why not say it as it is? – the bodies of huge numbers of women, children, horses, donkeys, camels, yes, even dogs . . . A terrible book could be written about the episodes I heard tell of the following morning alone, of what had been enacted during the two or three hours the reprisals lasted . . .

Fromentin didn't write that book. He deleted the lieutenant's story from his manuscript and contented himself with a summary: 'They waded in blood; there were corpses by the hundred.'

In Fromentin's writing, too, there is a contrast between surface and depth, between what the eye sees up there and the actual circumstances further down. In one place in the manuscript he asks: 'A third of the population killed – with what right, because of what crime or what threat and with what doubtful results?'

But he at once stops himself: 'I have no right either to describe or to judge a victory of this kind.'

Nor did he try. He deleted the passage. He blamed the silence in Laghouat on the climate. It became romanticism.

44

The survivors of the massacre had fled south. Some returned and were then directed to inferior neighbourhoods, all their possessions confiscated, and the entire booty of mats, weapons, jewellery and clothes removed. 'All the houses from the poorest to the wealthiest are empty,' Fromentin writes.

Under such circumstances, it was not easy to exercise the traditional Arab hospitality towards a travelling Frenchman. All the prerequisites were lacking.

Fromentin touches on the truth when he says that two societies confront each other in Laghouat: 'One has power and words. The other is a master of silence.'

Rhetorical phrasing. The lieutenant expresses himself more clearly:

> It is impossible to know how long the desire for revenge
> will live on, *he says*. I could swear that when the day of
> reckoning eventually comes, it would give them great
> pleasure to fill my belly with small stones or flay me
> alive to make a drum out of my skin.

At night the silence is broken by the howls of dogs who had fled the massacre to a rock outside the town. It proved impossible either to get them to return or to drive them away. As long as they had plenty of food on the battlefield or in the burial places, all was calm. But then the dogs turned more and more wild and began to attack passers-by like wolves.

Today, in the chapel dedicated to Sidi el-Hadj Aissa, there are the following words: *Death is the door through which we all have to go.*

True. But those faced with imperialism often had to go through it somewhat in advance.

Fromentin in 1841. (*Daguerreotype by L.A. Bisson* fils. *Private collection, descendants of Eugène Fromentin*)

Eugène Fromentin, *Self-portrait*, early 1840s.
(*Private collection, descendants of Eugène Fromentin*)

After the conquest of Laghouat, the French threw corpses down the wells to punish the town.

They had never even considered remaining there themselves. No one had dreamt a garrison would be placed so far south.

But General Pelissier decided to keep Laghouat. The French became prisoners of the town.

They were to live there. They had to have water.

To clean the wells, well-workers were conscripted from other oases. They belonged to the lowest stratum of the desert's black proletariat. Only slave workers could be forced down into wells turned into graves.

Down there, the dead bodies had swollen with the gases of decay and were pressed against the well walls. The corpses were so firmly wedged in, they had to be levered apart.

Their flesh had begun to dissolve, the bodies disintegrating. The poisoned water became a mess of remains of corpses into which the well-divers were forced deeper and deeper.

The water-table in the northern part of the town was six metres below the surface, in the southern part twelve metres. The largest of the wells contained 256 corpses, not counting the bodies of animals.

This was something no one wanted made public. But nor did anyone try to hide it.

That year, in 1853, modern racism was born with de Gobineau's *Essay on the Inequality of Human Races*. Also in the bookshops was Herbert Spencer's *Social Statics* in which social Darwinism was launched, some years before Darwin produced biological Darwinism.

The French officers in North Africa could scarcely have

known about that. But they were children of their age. Some thought it, others did it.

And it was not the first time, far from it. The history of imperialism is a well full of corpses.

In Laghouat, the wells were confiscated and for the rest of the century remained under military administration. In the future, they would be cleaned out by the same black well-divers and their children, grandchildren and great-grandchildren.

To Ain Sefra

46

I drive westwards from Laghouat. The road follows the Atlas Mountains: empty grandstands facing the endless football pitches of the desert. Signposts indicate direction and give distances straight out into the gravel – but I see no other route apart from the one I am taking.

'Long hours of emptiness, nourished by silence,' in the words of Isabelle Eberhardt.

In Sweden, when trying to imagine the desert, I thought of sandy beaches which never reach the water. But it is fairly rare to see beaches in the desert, which is more like an endless schoolyard: a vast, hard-packed desolation extending without end towards the horizon.

Some rocks are left behind, alone on the bare ground. They were too heavy. The light ones have gone. Everything that can has fled.

Fromentin's success with *A Summer in the Sahara* tempted many writers to follow in his footsteps. Daudet, Gautier, Maupassant, even Flaubert, all travelled in Africa and had a relationship with the desert.

But the ultimate heir to Fromentin's romanticism is Pierre Loti.

Both came from the French Atlantic coast – Fromentin from La Rochelle, Loti from Rochefort. Between these two towns lies a water-logged marshy area sliced through by brim-full ditches and canals, the ebb-tide exposing muddy river banks. The oyster beds overflow like Chinese rice paddies, the farmland sticky, the water flourishing and stagnating in the pools.

A landscape completely opposite to the desert. In addition, Loti was a naval officer, the sea his profession. But he had the desert within him.

In Fromentin's life, the desert was more or less chance. In Laghouat, he accidentally found out things he never dared tell and shrouded them all in mystery, which attracted the general public. Success created a demand for his desert images, and they kept him busy, earning him a living for the rest of his life.

Loti's desert romance is no chance. It is part of a mendacity running far deeper, embracing his whole personality.

A small boy was once given a miniature landscape by his elder brother. All through his childhood he continued to add to this wonderful landscape, which extended into a whole little world where every stone and every butterfly was charged with fantasies.

When the boy left his childhood home, he locked up his museum and sealed the door, locking in his childhood. Time was not to be allowed.

By then disaster had already struck the family. First his beloved elder brother died. Then his father was charged with embezzlement, lost his job and crawled like a rat along the walls of the houses in Rochefort. The money for which the father had been responsible had to be repaid, the family sank into poverty, the childhood home was sold, the father died and the only son took on the debt.

This is how he became a writer. This is when he adopted the pseudonym of Pierre Loti.

Fifteen years later, when everything has been paid off, he asks his ship's watch to wake him *once an hour* to tell him he is free of debt.

When his success as an author has made him rich, he buys back the parental home and turns it into a museum of fantasy, into a world in miniature. The façade remains untouched, but he rebuilds the interior according to his exotic dreams. The old quarters are filled like a honeycomb with the different rooms of his writing: the Turkish room, the Gothic, the Renaissance salon, the Japanese room, the Chinese, the Egyptian . . .

One room alone is left untouched. It is the smallest of them all, squeezed between the Chamber of Mummies and the

Turkish room. It is bare, but not, like the bedroom, for calculated effect. It is simply an ordinary little French study with a
black chair and a black desk.

This is where Loti worked. Here he wrote a great many of
his forty books, at the same desk at which his father once did
his accounts.

All around this sober little room was the scenery of his life.
Few authors have had such a need to enter their dreams and
inhabit them. To write a book set among Basque smugglers, he
does not just live with them: he takes his Basque clothes and
weapons home with him, has the back of the compound
equipped as two Basque rooms and sends for an unknown
Basque woman who bears him two Basque children. After
work every day, he goes and plays with them for a little while.

But his existing wives, both the one at the front of the compound and the one at the back, mean less to him than the
heroine in his first novel, *Aziyadé*. Every evening he retreats
into his private mosque and spends several hours dreaming
and weeping at her tombstone. The dead increasingly fill his
existence – parents, relatives, favourite animals, all buried
beneath the courtyard of his childhood home, incorporated
into the museum of his life. His museum of death.

It started when he locked away his childhood. Then he
locked away everything else bit by bit. He wanted to preserve,
perpetuate, to prevent every change.

No wonder Loti loved the desert. In the desert all changes
have already occurred. Nothing grows, nothing dies, nothing
decays. Everything has gone. Only eternity remains.

The flatter the desert, the more you become imprisoned and locked in by the horizon. You welcome every movement that elevates you and provides a view. You welcome every interruption: hills with hard peaks like the neck of a broken bottle; great movable yellow boulders; or quite simply distant heights coloured milky white or pale blue by the distance.

This morning I saw a *marabout*, the sepulchre of a holy man, its distant white walls reflecting the light like a beacon.

It takes about an hour to climb up to the stillness and solitude. There is nothing there.

Nothing but a few lizard tracks in the sand.

Nothing but a few unglazed, cracked and crumbling jars, the tombstones of the poor.

Nothing but a few large split palm trunks, grey with age, their timber like pressed straw.

And then the *marabout* door glowing acid-green and sulphur-yellow in the morning sun.

Far down below, a man is hacking away in the dry riverbed and some dark men are spreading out their dark, moist dates to dry beyond a low mud wall.

I go down to them, where it is already hot in the sun. But when they greet you, the men's hands are still cool, almost cold – as if the night had remained behind in their bodies.

The only language we had in common was our hands.

Throughout his life, Pierre has himself photographed in ever more handsome costumes. He holds his head thrown back, thrusting out one leg in order to appear taller than he is.

That is when you see how small he is. And how that tormented him.

He walks on tiptoe in high-heeled shoes. His wives are made to measure, smaller than he is himself. To be on the safe side, his mistresses are of 'lower race'.

As a child, he read with thumping heart the letters from his admired older brother, Gustav, a ship's doctor who took a 'wife' in Tahiti. On his first trip abroad, Loti goes to Tahiti and looks up his dead brother's woman. The love of a brother, just as the little boy back home dreamt about, becomes the constantly recurring paradigm in his life and his art.

Again and again he writes the same novel. It is about a white man, often a naval officer, who has a romantic relationship with a woman of alien race or culture. She looks up to him as a higher being. Their love is estrangement, passion, departure. They part with pain, doomed to eternal longing for their lost paradise.

Once only does he fall in love with a Frenchwoman. He proposes and is turned down.

In the diary he kept with a bookkeeper's thoroughness all his life, these are the only pages missing.

That is when he becomes a bodybuilder. He can't change his height, but he can build up his muscles. He becomes an athlete and appears in a circus in close-fitting tricot.

Loti as a Turkish gentleman. (*House of Pierre Loti, Rochefort, France*)

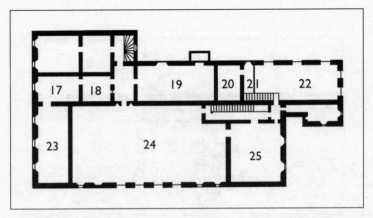

Second floor. 17: Gustave's study. 18: Arabic room. 19: Turkish room. 20: museum of Loti's childhood. 21: gallery of the Gothic room. 22: second storey of the Gothic room. 23: Chamber of Mummies. 24: Mosque. 25: Loti's bedroom.

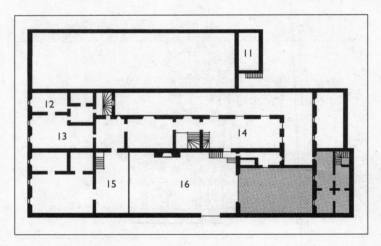

First floor. 11: terrace onto the garden. 12: Loti's childhood bedroom. 13: Room of Bees. 14: Gothic room. 15: gallery of the Renaissance room. 16: second storey of the Renaissance room.

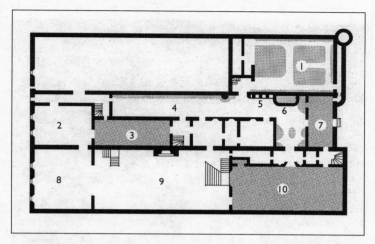

Ground floor. 1: garden. 2: Red room. 3: Japanese pagoda. 4: court-yard. 5: cloister. 6: fountain. 7: Rural room. 8: Blue room. 9: Renaissance room. 10: Chinese room.

Areas in grey no longer exist.

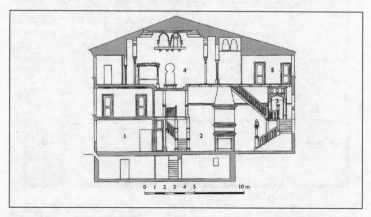

1: Blue room. 2: Renaissance room. 3: entrance to the Gothic room. 4: Mosque. 5: Loti's bedroom.
(*Phillipe Oudin; House of Pierre Loti, Rochefort, France.*)

Loti as a circus performer. (*House of Pierre Loti, Rochefort, France*)

Loti as a naval officer. (*House of Pierre Loti, Rochefort, France*)

Loti as the goddess Osiris. (*House of Pierre Loti, Rochefort, France*)

With a certain satisfaction, I regard the body I have
created with my exercises. The muscles stand out in
relief in the close-fitting costume. An old juggler
elevates the effect by lightly shading in the contours of
my muscles with a pencil. This strange anatomical toilet
takes twenty minutes.

Even in his nakedness he has to disguise himself. He dyes his
moustache and rouges his cheeks; he sits in the French
Academy made up like an old whore – hoping no one will see
how small he is.

He loves his way through the world, conquering it in the
form of women. Asia, Africa, the South Seas and the Atlantic,
the deserts of Sahara, Sinai and Persia – he has been everywhere, he has skimmed the romanticism off existence and
taken it back with him into his art and home.

In his doll's house, the world at last is given its correct pro-
portions. Inside it, he is large.

51

A moon-pale and determined young woman has been given an
assignment by the French Academy to free Pierre Loti from
his enchanted house. The Academy Action Group arrives in a
helicopter and those most immortal climb down rope ladders
onto the roof of the mosque. They search through the house
without finding Loti. 'Search thoroughly,' says Isabelle. 'He's
always in disguise.' But they find nothing but a little dog
which she takes in her arms as she climbs up into the roaring

helicopter, its rotor blades making the roof tiles jump. The dog is a small black and white Scottie with a bristly moustache and yearning eyes. One of its hind legs is rather stiff from being almost constantly raised. It also carries its nose very high.

'You can see it's Pierre Loti's dog,' says Isabelle. Then the disguise suddenly falls away and little Loti is standing there with his nose in the air – without his dog-mask, but strangely dog-like all the same.

52

More people drown in the desert than in the sea. They drown from lack of imagination. They simply cannot imagine enough water to drown in.

An *oued* is a dried-out river channel. But it could be thousands of years since any river flowed there, so it is more correct to say that an *oued* is the track left by torrents that have passed by. The desert is full of tracks of that kind, and you can live a whole life without ever seeing them filled with water. It is like living by the main line south without ever seeing a single train. Gradually you begin to think none will come. And if the whole landscape is a shunting-yard full of similar railway lines where no trains run, either – well, then you finally feel absolutely safe.

When the express train comes thundering along one night in accordance with some unknown timetable, you are not prepared. The torrent suddenly roars through and drowns everything in its path.

It came to Ain Sefra on the night of October 21, 1904.

I admit that I cross the *oued* in Ain Sefra with some haste. I can see bits of skeleton in the sand on the other side. And further up, whole corpses of sheep, goats and cattle – swept down by a tidal wave? Or is it a kind of animal cemetery?

I come to a forest planted to bind the dunes. A shepherd is reading a book there.

'Sidi Bou Djema?' I say, in monosyllables.

He points to the faint outline of a wall on top of a dune and replies equally monosyllabically:

'Sidi Bou Djema!'

But when I get up there, it is just a wall enclosing a small garden where a lone man and his dog grow chickpeas and onions.

The man is very friendly and he speaks beautiful French. He knows exactly where the tomb is and is pleased to take me there.

It is his garden. He laid it out himself. He dug the well himself, eleven metres deep. He fired the clay bricks for the wall himself. It would have been ready by now if it hadn't rained the other day. His semi-fired bricks have run out into the ground – look at this! Now he has to start all over again. He is used to that. He was a guest-worker in France for eight years and has worked in Marseilles and Lyons. He has even been to Paris. Now he has come back, has a wife and six children, five of them boys, and he is looking forward to a secure old age when he no longer needs to do any work, other than potter around in his garden.

As he is telling me this, we have got as far as the burial ground of Sidi Bou Djema. It lies with dunes and mountains behind it and a view over the *oued* where it happened.

A few spindly stems of grass grow in the sand after the rain. But all the same, it is a very desolate place. The desolation seems to be concentrated on the absurd buckled aluminium saucepan hanging at the back of a tombstone. On the front it says in European letters:

ISABELLE EBERHARDT

54

The act of departure is the bravest and most beautiful
of all. A selfish happiness perhaps, but it is happiness –
for him who knows how to appreciate it. To be alone, to
have no needs, to be unknown, a stranger and at home
everywhere and to march, solitary and great, to the
conquest of the world . . .

That is what Isabelle Eberhardt writes in a piece sometimes called 'The Road', sometimes 'Notes in Pencil'.

Departure is a tradition in her family. Her surname comes from her German maternal grandmother, Fräulein Eberhardt, who left her country to live with a Russian Jew.

Her mother marries an old Russian general, but then leaves him to go to Geneva with the children's young tutor – a handsome, intellectual Armenian, Tolstoy's apprentice, Bakunin's friend. He has been a priest, is married and now leaves his wife and children to live with his beloved in exile.

He teaches Isabelle six languages: French, Russian, German, Latin, Greek and Arabic. But he never admits to her face that he is her father.

She grows up among exiled anarchists in a chaotic milieu in which catastrophe is the natural state.

When she is eight, her brother Nicholas joins the Foreign Legion.

When she is nine, her sister Olga runs away and marries against the will of her family.

When she is seventeen, her favourite brother Augustin joins the Foreign Legion.

When she is twenty, she goes with her mother to Algeria. They both convert to Islam. The mother dies and is buried in Annaba.

When she is twenty-one, her brother Vladimir commits suicide.

When she is twenty-two, she gives her father, who is dying of cancer, an overdose of a pain-killing drug which, intentionally or not, ends his life.

She is alone in the world. At the turn of the century in 1900 she writes in her diary that the only form of bliss, however bitter, destiny will ever grant her is to be a nomad in the great deserts of life.

55

In secret, my sister Isabelle winds wet cotton bandages round her chest. She wears these bandages under her clothes and with not the slightest sign betrays what is going on. Only I know about it and I cannot stop her. She winds the wet bandages tightly, tightly round her chest. When they dry and shrink, they slowly crush her chest and suffocate her heart. No one can save her.

56

'From where have I got this morbid craving for barren ground and desert wastes?' Isabelle Eberhardt asks.

In her teens, she was charmed by the melancholy escapism of Loti's first novel *Aziyadé*, and he became her favourite author. When his *The Desert* came out in 1895, she was eighteen years old. Two years later she set out into the desert on her own for the first time. Loti was the one she always took with her on her journeys, the only person she looked up to as a forerunner and example.

She thought she had found her soulmate. He had a beloved older brother who had gone to sea, she has a beloved older brother who became a legionnaire. Her life, like his, is shrouded in departure and loss. Both live in disguise. And both love the desert, where they see their emptiness and their longing for death take shape.

Eberhardt as a Bedouin.

Eberhardt as a spahi.

Michel Vieuchange set off into the desert disguised as a woman. Isabelle sets off into the desert disguised as a man.

To her it is not just a disguise. The French language mercilessly reveals whether the writer considers him- or herself to be a man or a woman. Even in her diary Isabelle uses the masculine to describe herself.

Pierre Loti disguised himself as an Arab, but also as a Chinese, a Turk and a Basque. In every harbour, in every book, he takes on a new disguise. He became a cut-out doll for ever in new costumes, a cultural chameleon melting into every environment and lacking authenticity wherever he went.

The disguise goes deeper in Isabelle. When she returns to Africa, she wants to free herself from her past and take on a new and Arab identity. She becomes the Tunisian author Si Mahmoud Essadi.

Dressed in the clothes of an Arab man, she sets off into the desert. She has been waiting for this moment all her life. She rides between the oases with a few native cavalrymen, with a group of legionnaires, with a *chaamba* caravan, with an African on his way home to his village to get a divorce. She writes:

Now I am a nomad – with no other homeland than
Islam, with no family, no one in whom to confide,
alone, alone for ever in the proud and darkly sweet
solitude of my own heart . . .

She soon finds a separate confidant in one of her Arab lovers. Slimene Ehni is a sergeant in the native cavalry. She meets him in El Oued and through him becomes a member of a Sufi community, which is secretly opposed to French rule.

Another Arab fraternity closer to the French tries to murder her. A stretched washing line softens the blow and saves her life.

The French army banish her from North Africa and she ends up in Marseilles, where she supports herself for a while by writing letters in Arabic for the guest-workers.

Slimene also goes there, and on October 17, 1901, they marry. By marrying an Arab in the service of France, she becomes a French citizen and can return to the desert.

With Slimene she rents a small house in Ain Sefra, which is the headquarters of the French troops during the 'pacification' of the border with Morocco.

Even as Madame Ehni, she wears men's clothes and continues her androgynous life beside camp fires and in soldiers' brothels. Only the male rôle provides her with the freedom to ride around reporting for the newspaper *l'Akbar* in the Sahara, which the French are just conquering. Only the male rôle gives her the freedom to make love with anyone, to drink anisette with the legionnaires and smoke kif in the cafés, where she shocks listeners with her expositions on the pleasures of brutality and the voluptuousness of subjection.

58

I push my way through a thick dark desert of trees which is called 'forest'. I am in a hurry and must not come too late. In the end the forest opens up into a clearing. I see a figure hanging by the feet from a branch and I rush over. It is Isabelle! Her normally moon-pale face is blue-black and contorted. I cut her down and carefully arrange the dead body on the ground.

59

The Globe, a sports arena in Stockholm, is transformed from a descending hot-air balloon into a diving bell. Isabelle and I are sluiced out into the water, spouting cascades of pearly bubbles from our oxygen masks. But very soon we are forced to go back as if into a womb. We have been born into an element that is not ours, in which we do not belong, in which we cannot live – except for short moments with the piece of bitumen between our teeth.

60

'The thought of death has long since been familiar to me,' wrote Isabelle towards the end of her life.

Who knows? Perhaps I shall soon let myself slip into it, voluptuously and without the slightest worry. With time I have learnt not to look for anything in life but the ecstasy offered by oblivion.

Pierre Loti lived with his death-wish until he was seventy-three. Isabelle Eberhardt only lived to twenty-seven. By then she had

Eberhardt seated, cigarette in hand, about six months
before her death, 1904.

no teeth, no breasts, no menstruation, was as thin as a well-diver, and almost always depressed. 'If this foray of mine into the darkness does not stop, what will be its terrifying outcome?'

Her life was an extended suicide. With increasing regularity she took refuge in drugs, alcohol and a brutal, self-destructive, indiscriminate sexuality. She suffered from innumerable ill-nesses, among them malaria, and probably syphilis.

At her own urgent request, she was discharged from the hospital in Ain Sefra on October 21 and returned to her house by the *oued*.

The torrent that drowned her came that night.

61

When Isabelle died, her first novel, *Vagabond*, was just being serialized in *l'Akbar*. Her sketches and short stories had often been included in Algerian newspapers. A large number of manuscripts was saved from the flood.

The editor-in-chief of *l'Akbar*, Victor Barrucand, published a selection in 1906. Quite well-meaningly, he had first prettied up her texts.

She wrote: 'Everyone laughed.' He added: 'People laughed at his rusticity; his gesture was that of a shepherd.'

She wrote: 'Freedom was the only happiness accessible to my nature.' That sounded too simple. He improved on it: 'Freedom was the only happiness that was necessary for my eager, impatient and yet proud nature.'

Despite the revisions, the book was a success and Barrucand continued to publish Isabelle's manuscripts in 1908, 1920 and

1922, by then with greater respect for the integrity of her writing. The diaries and other writings she left were published in 1923, 1925 and 1944 by R-L Doyon. Grasset began to publish her collected writings in 1988. Most of these editions also contain short biographies. More extensive biographies have been published in France, Algeria, England and in the USA in 1930, 1934, 1939, 1951, 1952, 1954, 1961, 1968, 1977, 1983, 1985 and 1988.

62

What is it about Isabelle Eberhardt that goes on fascinating generation after generation?

I have plenty of time to think about that as I drive on through the desert.

She did not write nearly so much as her master, Pierre Loti. As a rule, nor did she write so well. And yet she is the one to survive. Why?

'One must never look for happiness,' she writes. 'One meets it by the way – always going in the opposite direction.'

There is a great deal of sparkling use of words in her work. It is not the average that counts. It is the highlights.

It is not the quantity that counts, it is the totality. And that applies not only to her language, but also body language. The gesture of life.

Isabelle dressed in male clothes and dived into the wells of the Saharan Arab world. At the same time, Jack London was putting on working clothes and letting himself sink into *People of the Abyss* (1903).

Eberhardt on horseback. (*Painting in oils by G. Rossegrosse*)

He was conducting a social experiment. He wanted to experience with his own body what wretchedness means for the truly poor.

Isabelle was doing the same. But with no secret gold coin sewn into her waistband. She dived without any safety rope. She went undercover with no return.

The boundaries she crossed were not only social, but racial. A white woman in the American South openly preferring black men as lovers and marrying one of them without altering her unbridled life – considered in those terms, it is easier to understand what forces Isabelle was challenging.

The French Empire in North Africa rested ultimately on the myth of the superiority of the white race. Her whole way of life questioned that myth.

It also questioned the myth of male superiority. If a female transvestite could penetrate the world of men and acquire its freedoms, vices and privileges, then the gender rôles were made to waver. Unclear sexual identity aroused anxiety and aggression. Isabelle put herself outside all categories.

Even that might possibly have been forgiven, as her fate verified all prejudices, apparently confirming that anyone who defies the conventions sinks into the dregs. So far, so good. But throughout her deterioration, Isabelle had the insolence to maintain a sense of moral superiority. That was unforgivable.

In that respect she belongs to a totally different family from Loti. She belongs to a long line of French literature running from Villon via Baudelaire and Rimbaud to Céline and Genet. She may be the only woman in that company.

The Immoralist

63

André Gide's *Fruits of the Earth* was published in Swedish in 1947, when I was fifteen.

As soon as I opened the book I felt someone was speaking to me, not over my head to other adults, but directly to me. And so confidentially, almost whispering, as if it were late at night when everyone else was asleep.

The book gave me another name, Natanael, which drew me into the text so that we could be together there. I liked it very much.

Some writers hide themselves in Action, others conceal themselves in Facts. But the master in *Fruits of the Earth* despised such hiding places. He talked about himself. He had a message. It filled the whole book. It was already there in his voice, in his way of speaking to me.

I was looking for a Master. I heard his voice for the first time in *Fruits of the Earth*, and fortunately he was also looking for what I wanted to be: an apprentice.

That was dangerous and forbidden. I realized that at once. The Master defied all authority. He preached departure, departure from everything, even from himself. He said: 'When you've read my book, throw it away and go out! I would like it to have given you the desire to leave something, anything, your town, your family, your way of thinking. Don't take my book with you . . . Forget me.'

That voice made me happy. But it also frightened me, made me afraid of the demands it made, afraid of the great unknown awaiting me.

64

'Our actions consume us, but they give us our radiance.'

That could be an epitaph for Isabelle Eberhardt.

She went to North Africa in 1897, when *Fruits of the Earth* was on sale for the first time. She died in 1904 when *The Immoralist* had just been published. Her whole writing life was lived between these two of Gide's books.

She was obsessed by the same mystique of departure as Gide. She preached the same nomadism. As he did, she wanted to try every experience, even those that were bad, brutal or depraved. It is conceivable that the reason why she dressed as a boy was in order to become his favourite apprentice, Natanael.

But there is nothing to indicate that she read Gide, at that time still a little-known young writer. André and Isabelle were simply children of the same day.

And through *Fruits of the Earth*, that day also became mine.

65

I came to *Fruits of the Earth* from *Manual for Infantrymen*, which had long been my favourite book. I also came from the training guide *Physical Fitness and Strength*. I read Gide in the same way. I came from *Scouting for Boys*. In this last, the narrative and descriptive parts were interspersed with small comments in brackets: '(practise it!)'. I read parentheses of that kind into *Fruits of the Earth* as well.

When it said:

'Every creature is capable of authenticity, every feeling of fullness.'

Or:

'I lived in a state of almost uninterrupted, passionate surprise.'

Then I also read the invisible words 'Practise it!'

Passionate surprise . . . ?

I loved my father, but had he ever been passionate? Did he even know what the word meant?

Within me was a boundless need to be seized and elevated. Everything around me denied that need. Only in *Fruits of the Earth* was it understood: 'Never stop, Natanael. As soon as an environment has become like you, or you like your environment, it is no longer any use to you. Then you must leave it. Nothing is more dangerous to you than *your* family, *your* room, *your* past.'

Was I getting like my father? Would I become the Secretary of the Älvsjö branch of the Swedish Red Cross, as he was? Would I dilute my milk with water to spare my stomach? Would I live without travelling, without festivities, without thinking, without adventures?

'Families, I hate you!' says Menalces. Through a window, he sees a boy sitting reading beside his father. The next day Menalces meets the boy on his way back from school. The next day they talk to each other, and four days later 'he left everything to come with me'.

The biblical associations with the Apostles who left everything to follow the Master gave me the courage to abandon myself to such dreams: one day Someone would walk past in the November darkness out there on Långbrodal Road, Someone would see me though the window where I was bored to death doing my homework beside my father, and this Someone would call out to me and take me out into the great wide world outside Älvsjö.

We would wander in that fatal moonlight over the desert. We would walk barefoot on smooth blue rocks, our eyelids cooled by the night.

We would see the walls of desert cities turning red towards evening and glowing faintly on in the night – deep walls in which the midday light is stored. At night, they slowly repeat what the day has taught them.

We would see Bou Saada. We would see Biskra. 'Over the moonlit terraces in Biskra, Meriem comes to me through the tremendous silence of the night. She is entirely enveloped in a torn white haik which she laughingly lets fall as she stands there in the doorway . . .'

After every sentence of that kind, I read with racing heart a secret *Practise it! Live it!*

Bou Saada, 'the fortunate town', lies in a hollow between three mountains. Its fortune is that its wells are connected to an underground lake constantly supplied with fresh water from the three mountains. The old wells can be thirty metres deep and irrigate twenty-four thousand date palms.

Today the basis of the economy is not dates but oil. The powerful desert vehicles of the prospectors, covered in mud and sand, stand outside the Hotel Caida. The oil men swill beer in a bar like a swimming baths, their voices echoing between tiled walls. They gather noisily around the long tables in the dining room with their big laughs and big wallets. A small plate of soup and a mess of vegetables costs as much as a dinner at the luxurious Opera Cellar in Stockholm.

Exchange rates create the image of the Foreigner. If the Foreigner is to appear powerful, rich and generous, then there has to be an exchange rate which makes everything cost about half what the Foreigner pays back home. If the Foreigner is to appear powerless, poor, stingy and complaining, then there has to be an exchange rate such as there is in Algeria.

I am staying at the Hotel Transatlantic. When it opened in 1909, the Foreigner was rich and powerful. Then the water closets flushed, hot water rushed out of the taps from Jacob Delafont & Co in Paris, the piano was properly tuned, the lights in the chandeliers sparkled, the Ouled Nail girls danced and made love. Those were the days.

Fruits of the Earth speaks with rapture about these girls. Loti wrote a whole book about them. Maupassant praises them. He came across them at the Café Joie in the main square and spread the rumour all over Europe that their wantonness was all part of the Ouled Nail tribal culture. According to ancient custom, the girls lived those happy days as prostitutes to save enough for their dowries.

Today, the Transatlantic in Bou Saada is the only surviving hotel of a chain that once stretched across the whole of North Africa. An infinitely old man shows me up the high stairs, as narrow and steep as a ladder. A yellow plastic bucket in the bath has to serve as both shower and WC. The beds are as cold and deep as graves.

67

I am lying on the ground in a strange town. A crowd of children dressed in white see me and come running over. They stand around me, chattering in French to each other, bending down and touching me, plucking at my clothes, touching my skin, lifting my hand. I am tremendously frightened. I expect them to say:

'He's dead.'

I don't know myself whether or not I'm alive .

68

In the morning, the infinitely old man has put on a once-white jacket and from the narrow spout of an enamel pot pours a bubbling, pale brown drink which could well be tea, may be coffee. His hands with their raised veins shake as he pours.

For five years after the death of my mother, I had my father's full confidence. Then he went behind my back and started seeing another woman.

The first time she visited us at home, as I was seventeen and was reading *Fruits of the Earth*, I suddenly felt terribly sorry for her.

Beside my old father, she seemed so young and lively, so unused. Did she really understand what she was letting herself in for? She didn't know what he was really like, as I did, from long experience.

After dinner, Father went out into the kitchen to fetch the coffee. Then I said: 'Surely you're not considering marrying someone who is already dead?'

She looked at me in horror.

'Ssh, he can hear what you're saying.'

I thought I had nothing to hide, and actually raised my voice as I went on. 'He hasn't read a book for fifteen years, or thought a new thought. Everything about him has solidified into clichés and routines. He's dead.'

As I was saying this, I saw from her expression that it was hopeless. I fell silent. Then my father, as old as I am now, came back into the room. He poured the coffee through the narrow spout of an enamel coffee pot. He didn't say anything. But I can still see before me his hands, with their raised veins, shaking as he pours.

Eventually, Someone really did walk past and see me. He was a British composer called John. I was pleased a grown man was interested in me and taking me seriously. In the summer of 1948, I went to London to stay for a few weeks with John in his flat.

It soon turned out that our expectations of this meeting were quite different.

'You're reading *Fruits of the Earth*,' John said. 'Do you see what your favourite book is about?'

He showed me one place after another, for example the bit in the sixth book about the dazzling light in the towns of the Orient. I had often read that. But clearly not thoroughly enough. I hadn't seen that among the white-clad Arabs were also children who appeared far too young, don't you think, to know anything about love? 'Some of them had lips hotter than newly hatched baby birds.'

'Practise it! Live it!' said John, and kissed me.

I was scared. I had no desire to be involved like that. As soon as I could, I escaped from the flat and ran through the streets of London to the Swedish Embassy, where, still gasping with the fear and effort, I rang the doorbell.

It was Sunday morning. A gigantic British butler gazed down at me blankly from the top stratum of society.

Haughtily, he saw me off.

It was pouring with rain. I had nowhere to go. I went back to John. When he found out where I had been, he was instantly transformed from attacker into victim.

'Are you crazy?' he said. 'Do you want me sent to prison?'

He told me about Oscar Wilde. Wilde was the prototype for Menalces in *Fruits of the Earth*.

I could hardly believe it.

'What had a poseur like Wilde to teach the master of honesty, André Gide?' I said.

'Wilde was world famous,' said John. 'The young André Gide had still not had anything published when they met in Paris in 1891. They were together every day for three weeks. Gide tore those three weeks out of his diary.

'The same year the master of honesty published *Fruits of the Earth*,' John went on, 'the master of poseurs left prison a broken man. That could happen to me, too, if you report me to the Embassy.'

Naturally, I didn't. John and I made a pact – he left me alone and I didn't go to the Embassy. But the message in *Fruits of the Earth* had suddenly shrivelled. I no longer called myself Natanael.

70

On the road between Bou Saada and Biskra is a small place called Zaatcha.

The name has never become as famous as Song My or Oradour-sur-Glane, but what it denotes is the same: massacre. The French razed the town to the ground after the rebellion of 1849 and the whole population was slaughtered, men, women and children.

Today the name denotes some dusty palm trees, a petrol station and a café rattling with dominoes. The morning bread has all gone and the evening bread has not yet arrived. There are three red plastic chairs and an iron one outside. I sit down to wait.

Out of old Swedish habit, I turn my face to the sun and roll up my sleeves to get a bit of tan on my arms.

People around me are surprised and upset. They look at me as if I were a flasher. In the Sahara, the sun is the Enemy just as much as it is the Friend with us. Sunbathing in the Sahara – it's something you simply do not do.

Not so long ago, the sun was suspect in Europe too. The first really immoral thing that happens in *The Immoralist* is that the main character takes all his clothes off in the sun. He sees some sunburnt workers and is himself tempted to undress. At first it feels cold and unpleasant. But the sun burns and after a while he is pleasantly roasted right through. 'My whole self lived in my skin,' he says.

Was he the very first modern sunbather? The sun, the liberator, teaches him not to be ashamed of his body, but to look upon it with delight. 'I felt harmonious and full of sensuality. I almost thought I was beautiful.'

Gide writes that when it was still regarded as more natural to burn down a village than to undress in public. Nakedness was characteristic of the inferior races, along with dark body colour. What was morally superior was white.

Sunbathing became a bold symbolic action, full of rebellion and hedonistic mystery:

It seemed to me, *Gide writes in* If It Die . . . , as if when lit through by the rays of the sun my body had undergone a chemical renewal. When I took off my clothes, it was as if all torments, restraints and worries ceased to exist. While my will melted utterly away, I let my body, now as porous as a honeycomb, secretively purify and prepare the honey flowing into the *Fruits of the Earth*.

Respectable people do not do such things. A respectable person burns down villages, but is careful not to let his will melt away.

The sun is scorching in Zaatcha. The evening bread has still not arrived. The houses are pale blue and honey-yellow. Some heavy long-distance trucks stop to fill up, surrounded by chattering mopeds. The children gather on the playground. The only thing that makes it a playground is the fence. No need for a sandpit. The wet salt desert smells of sea.

71

At the spa hotel in Biskra, I spend one night drinking with Wolfgang, a German desert fanatic crossing the Sahara on a motorcycle. *The Immoralist* is lying on the table in my room and Wolfgang says: 'The wife has a miscarriage, doesn't she? Otherwise she would have given birth to me.'

'You?'

'Yes, I grew up in exactly that kind of family. My friends thought I had the most wonderful father in the world. He thought so too. But he was interested in their opinion, not mine. True, he was full of charm and imagination. True, I admired him enormously. But he betrayed me over and over again – without even noticing. The book ought to be called *The Self-Absorbed*. In his world, the immoralist is the only person who really exists – that's what makes him immoral.'

It was one of those night-time hotel conversations which become absolutely honest only because both people are equally sure they will never have to meet again.

'Father was always very attentive towards my mother. But beneath the courtesies and tokens of love, the silence between them grew deeper and deeper, until finally it became explosive.

'They didn't dare separate. My father thought that without Mother, reality itself would cease to exist. Only she could nourish and sustain him. For her too, it was a matter of identity. There was nothing beyond their lifelong love, not even herself.'

'What happened?'

'One day when my mother was in the bath, he locked the bathroom door on the outside, went downstairs, poured petrol all over the living room and set fire to it. Then he went straight to the police and gave himself up. I almost think he expected praise. A respectable person does not separate from his wife, but one does have the right to burn down one's house, doesn't one? And it did indeed burn to the ground.'

'And your mother?'

'She was rescued at the last minute. I went to the Sahara. My father was a desert soldier in Rommel's army in the Second World War. He often told me about the desert when I was small. I had got it into my head that the solution to the mystery of him might be found here.'

I am staying in Beeskra and publishing the *Honey Bee Magazine* containing news from the beekeeper front seen entirely through the eye of the bee.

Even beesexual keepers get sharp criticism for what they

regard as beeneficial. But naturally I avoid exaggerated and unbeeleevable standpoints. Since the Bee Party came into power, the honey harvests have multiplied. That way the supply of sugar-water for the bees is assured. Continued co-operation with the beekeepers is naturally for the beeneefit of the bees.

The final 'libeeration', as we call it, is a central beetail that unfortunately has had to bee put off into the future.

73

From the main character's point of view, Gide's *The Immoralist* is a story of liberation.

Michel has recently lost his wife. Some of his friends travel to an oasis in the Sahara to meet him. Lying on his roof, they listen as he confides in them about his marriage.

He had married Marceline largely to please his father. During their honeymoon in North Africa, he finds out he is in the advanced stages of consumption. He has already given up and prepared himself for death when the sight of a small child suddenly gives him a strong desire to live.

His whole being begins to resist the disease. 'My health was my assignment. Everything that was wholesome was to be regarded as good, but I must reject and forget everything that did not heal.'

What arouses his will to live more than anything else is the company of children. When he sees them playing in Biskra gardens, semi-obliterated memories from his own childhood come into his mind. It amuses him to learn their games and arrange little parties for them with juice and cakes in his hotel room.

He begins to regain his strength. He experiences exactly the kind of jubilant re-entry into life described in *Fruits of the Earth*.

Soon he does not only want to regain his health, but to be strong and full-blooded. He seems to discover within himself a new creature which teachers, relatives, yes, even he himself had previously tried to suppress. He begins to see himself as something that can be perfected. 'Never has my will been more excited than in trying to achieve this unknown, still unclearly imagined perfection.'

He shaves off his beard and lets his hair grow. He sunbathes and exercises his body. But he doesn't dare, or doesn't want to share these experiences with Marceline. He wants to keep them to himself. He soon finds it both easy and amusing to lie to her and he also thinks these lies simply increase his love.

One day he rescues his wife from a drunken driver, and with his newly won strength thrashes the man. Then he makes love to her for the first time. She becomes pregnant, they return to France and settle on a country estate which had belonged to his mother.

Among intellectuals, Michel now feels himself a stranger. He thinks life, for him infinitely valuable, is nothing to them but an annoying hindrance to their writing. Instead he finds his way to a gang of semi-criminals and with them devotes himself to nightly thieving of his own possessions.

But Marceline falls ill and has a miscarriage. They leave the estate and travel south to find a place where she can regain her health.

'So once again I made an attempt to retain my love,' says Michel. But he no longer has any need of it. Happiness with Marceline is to him as superfluous as rest is to someone who is not tired.

He thinks he possesses within him untouched possibilities which are being suffocated beneath layers of culture and morality. Sins and crimes are acts of liberation. Evil is natural: 'In every living being the instinct for evil seems to me to be what is most immediate.' And everything which is natural should be affirmed: 'I feel nothing within me that is not noble.' So even what is evil is noble.

They leave the Swiss resort where Marceline has begun to regain her health. In the middle of winter, they travel south to seek sun and warmth. But Marceline simply gets worse. They finally arrive in Biskra. There he was saved. There she will also regain life!

The children in Biskra, who once gave him back the will to live and made him take the first step towards self-discovery, have become almost unrecognizable. 'Work, vice and indolence have left their mark on faces which two years ago radiated youth.' The boys have become dishwashers, road workers and butchers. 'How honest occupations brutalize!'

The only one to retain his beauty is a petty criminal, Moktir. Michel invites him to accompany him to Touggourt the next day. But Marceline is more ill than ever and, trembling, she presses up against Michel. He thinks:

'Shall I not stop? – I have sought and found my real worth: a kind of stubborn obduracy in wickedness (*le pir*). But how can I bring myself to tell Marceline that tomorrow we are going to Touggourt? . . .'

They take the mail carriage at dawn. Moktir is with them, happy as a king. The dismal road seems endless. Oases he thought would be smiling are wretched and he prefers the desert – 'the land of lifeless magnificence, of unbearable lustre.'

'You love what is inhuman,' says Marceline.

The scorching sand irritates her throat. The inhospitable landscape torments her. As soon as they arrive, she goes to bed. The rooms are terrible. She eats nothing. He makes tea for her, but the water is salty and tastes disgusting.

He leaves Marceline and disappears out into the night to Moktir's 'beloved' and makes love to her while her fiancé sits beside them playing with a rabbit. When he returns to the hotel, Marceline has her second lung haemorrhage. She dies that night.

He buries her in El Kantera, where he now lives a solitary and frugal life, making love sometimes with the beautiful dancer Meriem, sometimes with her little brother.

Have I done wrong? That is the question Michel asks his listeners on the roof terrace. In that case how did that wrong begin? Was it when I wanted to regain my health? Was it when I wanted to be strong? Was it when I wanted to be free? Why does this useless freedom I have gained now torment me?

We are not born human. We become that. We become that through solidarity with each other. We become that by taking responsibility.

That is the kind of person I wanted to be. I thought I was that kind of person.

Decisions are made in Paris. They are carried out in the Sahara. Then when the emotions that the name 'Smara' once inspired have vanished, the decision still remains.

I wanted to be Saint-Ex, the flyer who does not abandon a friend in distress in the desert.

I became Vieuchange, the desert wanderer who lies his way into continuing his journey, because he 'had wanted it, in Paris'.

The immorality in *The Immoralist* is not that Michel has changed. One has a right to be changed. The immorality is that he does not dare admit the change. He prefers to become a murderer rather than admit the new being within him.

Is it right then, as Eberhardt writes, that departure is the bravest and most beautiful of all actions?

It is far from always beautiful. But swallow your pride! Admit your defeat! If you have already secretly departed, then admit it – the sooner the better! Your most immoral actions are carried out in order to maintain the illusion of being moral.

The road between Biskra and Touggourt follows an underground flow of water called Oued Rhir. The wells that took their water from the *oued* were fifty to sixty metres deep.

The water carried with it sand and gravel which was removed by the well-divers, *ratassin*. They descended more than thirty metres below the surface of the water and worked there for between 90 and 160 seconds at a time. After completing their task, they were praised as heroes.

During his honeymoon, André Gide arrived in Touggourt on April 7, 1896. There he saw a man being let down to clean out a well sixty metres deep, lined with palm trunks.

'The effort required of these well-divers when they work under the water is incredible,' Gide writes. 'It is said that this man in particular was one of the bravest. He was rewarded with a medal. That evening he went insane.'

Anyone digging a fifty- to sixty-metre well must first get through the upper, unstable layer of sand. The shaft is lined with palm trunks and the space between the trunks filled with a mixture of clay and palm fibre to keep the loose sand out.

Often the well-digger must then get through several layers of polluted water before he reaches the sub-soil water. A watertight passage has to be made straight through the unclean water. Inside this passage, the well-digger works downwards through alternating firm and loose strata until he reaches the hard stone roof of the underground aquifer.

Then the foreman of the well-diggers, *mhallen*, descends to the bottom of the shaft and opens a hole through which the water spurts up and fills the well.

The Immoralist

In his journal from Touggourt, Gide says nothing about his wife's tears. But he describes the bitter taste of the water as it spurts up from the depths and fills the well.

77

Today, Touggourt receives me with high-tension cables, gas-ometers, construction cranes – the profile of the modern oasis. A small trickle of European desert maniacs gather at the Hotel Oasis.

Touggourt is the capital of the date world in the Sahara, the anchor in a chain of oases which produces one of the most famous quality dates in the world, 'Fingers of Light' – amber-coloured, almost translucent, with soft, moist and fragrant flesh.

But this is only one kind among thousands. There are date shops in which the vendors are swamped by dates of various kinds, various vintages, from various places, and as distin-guished in taste as French cheeses. Having tried only one kind of date, the kind imported into Sweden, is like having eaten only processed cheese from a tube.

Date wholesalers with gigantic warehouses and interna-tional distributors have mountains of dates of every colour – brown, yellow, black and red. Most of them are not the sticky Christmas kind, but dry and shrunken everyday dates. The people of the desert eat them like bread. They are often ground into flour. They are not sweet until right inside, by the stone.

Date traders have small stands of poles and sacking along-side the wise old men who sell herbal remedies and plant juices.

I see the white juice of *Launaea spinosa*, supposed to relieve headaches, but also used to exterminate rats. And the small brown angular seeds of *Peganum harmala*, an emetic which causes dreams of paradise. And henbane which is so common in the markets of the Sahara – used to relieve cramps and to dull pain as well as for its narcotic effect, but in larger quantities a deadly poison.

Different, apparently contradictory functions are combined in these modest bland substances. A few grains is the difference between intoxication and insanity, death and healing.

78

I make tea. It is so strong it's undrinkable. I make some more. That also blackens immediately. Where does the black come from? The answer is there. It is already in the water.

Two small girls are sitting on the floor picking lice out of each other's hair. The reason why they have lice is their arrogance at being human.

I visit a fort nearby. As I get closer, the imposing cannons turn out to be enlargements of old engravings, stuck on cardboard.

I find a note in my pocket which says *Canossa*. It refers to my divorce. I am being punished for my ignorant moralism. I thought those who could no longer love each other were just lazy. But work alone is not enough. Without grace, there is no love.

Michel has concluded his story. His friends remain lying silently on the roof beneath the stars.

Then the silence is unexpectedly broken by Marceline who is with them on the roof, concealed by the dark night.

'Now let me tell you what really happened,' she says. 'I didn't die in Touggourt, as Michel maintains. I'd had enough. I left him.

'Michel had married me to please his father. His mother died when he was fifteen and since then he and his father had lived in a very close and confident relationship. To the extent that the son acquired an old-fashioned air about him.

'He once said he had within him forces "which have retained all their secretive youthfulness". That was laughable coming from a twenty-five-year-old – but as I was married to him, I was able to refrain from laughing.

'After the wedding we went straight to his apartment in Paris, where two separate bedrooms were ready for our wedding night. His father's funeral and the wedding had exhausted Michel, and the honeymoon simply increased his exhaustion. In Tunisia he spat blood, and he arrived in Biskra unconscious. I had hoped to become a mother and found instead I was about to become a widow.

'That was why I loved the children in Biskra. Michel was angry at first, then more and more interested. To me he said with the conventional rhetoric of love: "Marceline, my wife, my life." But he didn't see me, he was looking past me at the Arab boy I had with me, at his tongue which was "rosy pink like a cat's", he said as he leant over and touched his narrow shoulder.

'He never touched me. But it was wonderful to see his will to live come back. He started eating again, he slept by the open window, and he was soon going out for walks with the children.

'During his entire recovery, he was much occupied with his own body. He sunbathed, exercised, looked at himself in the mirror with pleasure. I often wondered what moved inside him, but it appeared to be something vulnerable he wanted to keep to himself. By respecting his secrets – and even his lies – I hoped I would eventually gain his confidence.

'Sexually, I was still taboo to him. He appeared to be impotent. But once when I was out riding in a carriage, the driver had drunk rather too much and the horses bolted. Michel was beside himself with rage and thrashed the man, tied him up and took him back to town. More violence than the situation demanded, I thought; but it had an excellent effect on Michel's manhood. That night I became, as they say, "his".

'Perhaps it was that night which Michel always tried to live over again in our life together, though its reflection grew weaker and weaker for every repetition.

'Nonetheless, I managed to get pregnant. We returned to France and settled on an estate that had belonged to Michel's mother. Then suddenly he began to react to me like a child to his mother. He didn't see me as a fellow human being, but as an authority he had to defy, a supervisor he had to escape from.

'He couldn't remember his childhood, had never had any youth, and now he was slipping out into the woods night after night to partake in a kind of boyish adventure which would have been criminal if it hadn't been directed at himself. I pretended not to notice. I was absorbed in the expectation of the child – until my pregnancy was terminated by a miscarriage .

'When I was nursing Michel during his illness, I already knew, of course, that I was risking infection. And yet it came as a shock to me when I realized that I also had consumption.

80

'Now the tables were turned. Michel nursed me – with a tenderness his sick conscience made hectic and frightening. The more I needed him, the less he needed me. In the middle of his most tender care, he could exclaim: "I loathe compassion. All kinds of infections are concealed inside it. One ought not to feel sympathy for anyone but the strong!"

'Why shouldn't "one"? Because all compassion is as false and exaggerated as what Michel was now showing me? Because an unforced natural sympathy can only be aroused by the strong?

'That certainly isn't true of every "one". My own sympathy is aroused to its most irresistible by the frail and the vulnerable.

'It was because of that I loved Michel, who even in his newly won strength was so frail. I loved precisely what was vulnerable about him, what made him admire strength.

'"Now I understand your faith," I said. "Maybe it is beautiful, but it subjugates the weak."

'"That's just as it should be," he replied swiftly and involuntarily.

'It was horrible to feel the way he observed not only with "anxiety" but also with "expectation" the way my strength was fading. Full of consideration, he was forever taking me to new places which would be better for my health. But those exhausting journeys only took me closer to death – which Michel secretly had begun to long for as part of his own liberation.

'He wanted to go to Biskra. But his return was a terrible disappointment to him.

'Michel was fifteen when his mother died. That seemed to be a boundary he never crossed. As long as Charles, the bailiff's son, was fifteen, he interested Michel, but a year later he suddenly seemed foolish, ugly and indifferent.

'The same with the children in Biskra. Three years ago they had been under fifteen and delightful. Now they were simply repugnant.

'I begged him to stay in Biskra. He wouldn't listen. During the journey to Touggourt, he had eyes only for that boy prostitute fawning for his attention. I was a burden he was about to throw off.

'When he left me in that filthy, fly-blown hotel room and slipped out into the night, with an expression so secretive that it concealed nothing, I had suddenly had enough. I gathered up all my instinct for survival and left him for ever.

'Was that wrong of me? Could I have saved our marriage?

'If so, what should I have done? Can you see any possibility I didn't see?'

81

No, Marceline, I see no possibility.

I think at best your marriage could have been a mutual

pregnancy. Two people becoming pregnant with each other and finally giving birth to each other.

Some pregnancies last longer than others – the elephant's and the whale's. There are marriages which last for decades. But the aim is not to extend the pregnancy at any cost. The aim is that out of inevitable birth pains, two people will rise, each one freer and happier than they could be together.

In your case, there were not two people pregnant, but one. You gave birth to Michel. He could not do the same for you.

82

'In Africa and particularly in the Sahara, there are practically no signs of the presence of oil,' said Gulf's senior geologist in 1949. Seven years later, oil was gushing from a depth of 3,329 metres in Hassi Messaoud. Since then, the poverty-stricken Sahara has supported Algeria.

The road to Hassi Messaoud is lined with bits of black rubber, the corpses of giant tyres that once bore steel pipes, enormous caterpillar track front-loaders, and bulldozers.

Nearer the oil fields, the road crosses a marshalling yard of black oil pipes half buried in the yellow sand. The actual production area can be made out at a great distance, from the light of vast torches and the smoke rising over the horizon – they are burning off the gas, the pressure of which forces the oil up to the surface.

It is a perverse sight; hot flames against an already overheated sky, brilliant beneath a sun already providing more than enough light.

The town has a small square, with a few quick-growing trees and some concrete benches. The cool winter wind smells of sulphur.

Under a shared metal roof is a row of shop-huts, a small café where they sell a thin brown coffee-like drink and ochre-coloured lemonade, and a little post office where everyone ahead of me is surprised and embarrassed when I take my place at the end of the queue. They solve the problem by leaving. Soon I am at the head of the queue because I am the only one left.

The bookshop is advertising Rabia Ziana's new novel, *The Impossible Happiness* – an appropriate read for a night at the Hotel C.A.S.H. in Hassi Messaoud.

83

I crawl through the barbed-wire fence into a house which is at the same time half finished and an abandoned ruin. The barbs catch me. It's no use closing my eyes. It's no use covering my eyes. The light penetrates everywhere and so do the barbs.

Then a desert dune drifts in and covers the barbed wire. My lacerated eye sockets fill with flying soft warm sand. It is very pleasant. I was already blind. Now at last I can enjoy it.

André Gide went to North Africa for the first time in 1893. Twelve years earlier, the French had occupied Tunisia. Gide travels in Tunisia without mentioning the occupation. The conquest of Algerian Sahara is at its height. Gide does not mention it. In the occupied oases, military commanders rule like absolute monarchs and the Arab population is kept down with an iron hand. Gide sees nothing.

Others saw. Isabelle Eberhardt saw.

She was in North Africa while Gide was writing *The Immoralist*. She shows in her stories how France takes land from Arab small farmers, forcing them to work for the new French owners – who can't understand why their farm workers go around with such sly, sullen expressions.

She sees how those who object are taken away in chains to the prison in Tadmit. The guards force them to walk barefoot on the ridge of sharp stones formed between the wheeltracks on the road. 'With no verdict from the courts, punished by French administrators or local collaborators, with no chance of appeal, they are sent away to years of lonely suffering, with no hope of mercy.'

For Isabelle, like Gide, North Africa is primarily an erotic experience. When she falls in love with a young Tunisian, she leaves everything and goes with him, although he is a tax collector for the French. But her love affair does not stop her from seeing and reacting:

Everywhere among these poor, dark and recalcitrant tribes, we are given a hostile reception, *she writes*. Si Larb's good heart bleeds for them, and what we are

Gide at Biskra, 1893. (*Collection Roger-Viollet, Paris*)

doing – he out of duty, I out of curiosity – makes us ashamed as if we had committed an outrage.

There is no feeling in Gide that the conquest is an outrage. That doesn't come until the Congo books in the late 1920s. By then Joseph Conrad had taught him to see it.

Conrad and Gide were both in Africa in the early 1890s. Conrad was writing *Heart of Darkness* while Gide was writing *The Immoralist*. They were contemporaries – but it took Gide another thirty years to acquire Conrad's insight.

In *The Immoralist*, the moral conflict is enacted entirely between the husband Michel and the wife Marceline. The novel trembles with her unspoken reproaches and with his pride and shame when he discovers himself. Gide sees no other conflict.

85

'Nietzsche's small change' says the *Encyclopédie Universalis* contemptuously of *The Immoralist*.

Gide read Nietzsche, mad with jealousy at finding in him 'all his most secret thoughts'. An enormous Nietzsche moustache grew on Menalces' face, which had previously looked like Oscar Wilde's. It becomes a 'pirate face' and is given the famous Nietzschean gaze: 'a cold flame indicating more courage and determination than goodness.'

Gide, Saint-Exupéry, Vieuchange and Eberhardt – they have all looked into that gaze. All of them dive in after Nietzsche's small change.

The contempt, however, is unwarranted. Not until the vast wealth of high-flown rhetoric has been cashed into the ordinary small change of a household do we see what it really entails – for me, for you, for all of us.

86

So what was it actually all about?

Over the moonlit terraces, Meriem comes through the tremendous silence of the night, enveloped in a torn white haik.

'I am the "beautiful dancer" Michel lives with,' she says. 'Though, of course, this is a prettified circumlocution. My little brother Ali and I are prostitutes.

'Michel asks you: "Have I done wrong? How in that case did the wrong begin?"

'I reply: the wrong Michel does is naturally not that he wants to be healthy or strong or free. Nor is it that he is homosexual – we North Africans have always taken a more humane view of love between people of the same sex than you in Europe.

'What is shameful isn't there – but in the occupation, which makes love into prostitution and shrouds its crimes in myth.

'Maupassant saw my mother dancing in the Café Joie in Bou Saada. He was one of the first in Europe to spread the rumour about the wonderful wantonness of the Ouled Nail girls: they saved up their dowries by living life's happy days in the brothels.

'Similar legends are spread about the prostitutes in

Bangkok, for the same reason. Customers are given a moral alibi. The legends give an illusion of mutual desire to the exploitation of someone else's poverty.

'Isabelle Eberhardt was not deceived. In fortunate Bou Saada she wrote: "Never before have I been so well aware as here of the weight that hangs over all the occupied areas."

'Bou Saada had quite simply had the misfortune to be the first of the Saharan oases to be conquered by the French. After the conquest, the Ouled Nail tribe continued their resistance for another twenty years. When at last it ceased, the tribe was impoverished and their social network torn apart. War and occupation had led to social anarchy. With the misery also came prostitution, first around the garrisons, then around the tourist hotels.

'When the same thing occurred later in other oases, the legend had already made "Ouled Nail" into a brand name, used by all prostitutes regardless of which tribe they really came from. Many were children, who themselves had been led to believe the myth with which some of the greatest of Europe's writers marketed them.

'Michel's liberation presumes children "far too young, don't you think, to know anything about love?" It presumes child prostitution. That is the fundamental moral problem which is never put into words in *The Immoralist*.

'When my income is insufficient to support the family, my little brother Ali will have to let foreign gentlemen fuck his backside for money. That's what it is about. The rest is romanticism.'

'The journey is a door through which one goes out of the known reality and steps into another, unexplored reality, resembling a dream,' Maupassant writes in his travel accounts from Algeria.

Yes: the reality of the colonies functioned like a dream.

No one had asked the French officers to conquer Laghouat or Zaatcha. Far less had anyone asked the soldiers to massacre the population. No one forced them to do it. It was enough that no one stopped them. They were simply given an opportunity which they were unable to resist.

They took it – in the same way as Saint-Ex, Vieuchange, Loti, Eberhardt and Gide took the opportunity to step into their far more innocent dreams.

For them, the colonies were an arena in which they were able to *live out* everything not socially accepted in their own countries.

It is doubtful whether the colonies ever produced either the power or the income their supporters hoped for and advocated them in expectation of. But in the spiritual life of Europe, the colonies had an important function – as a safety vent, as an escape, a place to misbehave.

Like the dream, the colonies offered a refuge away from the demands of their own society, an outlet for the cruelty and self-importance not tolerated in Europe. Not yet tolerated.

In the colonies, while one represented the highpoint of civilization, it was possible to escape much of civilization's unpleasantness: the banality of the bourgeoisie, the *tristesse* of marriage, the inhibiting control of impulse – and become party to mass murder, child abuse, sexual orgies and other expressions of urges which at home largely found their outlets in dreams.

Maupassant alludes to it. Gide's *The Immoralist* is an indication of it. But apart from Conrad, of course, which of the writers of the epoch expressed it in art? Who is prepared even today to dive into this dark well and clean it out?

The Well-divers

88

Timimoun is the only oasis in the Sahara where I could imagine myself living.

I like the narrow winding alleys constantly changing direction to avoid the pursuing rays of the sun. The houses form bridges across the narrow shafts of streets, the streets becoming tunnels, the courtyards as deep as wells down which the sun cannot penetrate. The windows are narrow apertures, so deep the sun cannot shoot in through them. Over the centuries, innovations have built on the basic principle of desert architecture: defence against the sun.

I love the shimmering blue dragonflies hovering above the green flowering water of irrigation pools, a promising murmuring, rippling, gurgling everywhere. The water runs through a complicated system of gullies criss-crossing each other, branching out or merging. Black men plant cabbages in the soft silt.

I love the salt-white plains round Timimoun and the hour-glass fine sand. I love the mountains with their long red roots of sand. I love the new-moon dunes, shaped like sickles with sharp, wind-polished edges.

The car's shadow with its high wobbling wheels seems cut out of a comic strip as I return to Timimoun at sunset through a sea of dunes.

I would like to come back here always. I would like to spend the winters at the El Gourara hotel with my word processor and a small disc library of the classics of modern egoism from Hobbes to Huysmans. And soon all the other works 'on line' from all the national libraries and databases of Europe. Plus a discarded, bound and thumbed old desert novel by Pierre Loti.

That is my desert romanticism.

I would live here undisturbed by human complications, without love but also without pain.

Live off bread and dates, watching the wheatear and the desert crow, listening to the palm doves as they grumble, tut-tutting in the date grove. Sitting in the sunrise looking out over the salt marshes and enjoying the monotony and silence of the desert.

89

I have a bell. A copper sheep-bell. All round me in the great expanses of landscape I can hear the loud clanging of many different sheep-bells, some far off in the distance, others quite near.

Only my bell doesn't clang.

I feel inside it with my fingers and find a soft rag wound round the clapper.

It's a mangled, threadbare old towel, initials embroidered on it in blue, my mother's initials, which are also mine. I recognize the towel easily; as a boy, when I longed for love, I used to wrap it round my member and liberate myself into it.

90

A Swedish officer called Thorsten Orre wrote *Sketches from the Desert*, the first ever Swedish desert book, and he lived here in Timimoun.

I read Orre in the days when you could borrow two books 'for pleasure', but as many non-fiction, 'fact books', as you liked.

With this rationing system, Swedish libraries laid in my contemporaries the foundations of the often lifelong conviction that non-fiction was not 'for pleasure', that reality as an experience was always inferior to fiction.

Orre was one writer to help me out of that dogma. No fantasies ever matched his facts.

In a small village south of Timimoun, Orre met a man by the name of Abdelkader Ben Mohammed Omar, his professional title *rtass* – a thin, wretched thirty-year-old who looked fifty. He was also as good as deaf: both eardrums had been perforated. He was the last surviving well-diver.

Abdelkader undressed and tied a cloth around his hips, then greased his body with butter, stuffed tallowed camel wool into his ears and recited his prayer.

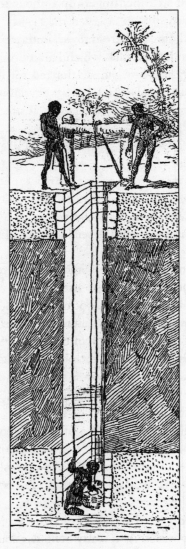

A well-diver at work.

The well to be cleaned was only eight metres deep. Orre measured the rope which fastened the basket. A heavy stone was put into the basket and lowered to the bottom. Abdelkader went over to the well and placed himself astride it, then thrusting his feet against the inside of the wall, he climbed down to water level.

There he took a deep breath, clapped his feet together and let himself sink.

The others stayed around the well, silent and grave. The work of the *rtass* is full of danger. He wears his life out in advance. Although a slave, or almost a slave, he is regarded as holy.

Orre stands with a watch in his hand. After twenty seconds of breathless silence, the rope begins to jerk as if someone were climbing up it. A cloud of bubbles rises to the surface and then Abdelkader's head appears.

He gets out of the well, wraps his *burnus* round him and watches in silence as the others hoist up the basket, now full to the brim with sludge from the bottom of the well.

He dives five times in a row that morning. In the afternoon, he again descends into the well and continues working. After his last dive, he goes to one side, dries himself thoroughly and sits down in the blazing sun with his back against a palm tree. His whole body is still shuddering.

91

I also shuddered.

I was afraid of wells. At Sunday School, I could hardly bear to listen when the brothers threw Joseph into the well. I looked down into the dark depths. I tasted the icy water. I sensed the absolute loneliness down there. I – who didn't even dare dive head first from the edge of the swimming pool – how could I read about the wells of the desert without becoming that diver myself?

It was always me, emaciated, marked by death, my eardrums already perforated from the tremendous pressure, who dived down to the bottom of the well to clean it out.

92

Götgat Hill has been transformed by the bulldozers into a deep shaft. I start climbing outside the milk bar at the foot of the hill. I am small but quite strong. I hold firmly onto the edge of the pavement and find good support for my feet from the stones and protruding iron girders. The situation looks hopeful.

But the pavement gets narrower, and by about halfway I am climbing directly on foundations of houses, like a façade climber, while at the same time the chasm below me grows deeper and deeper.

When the house foundations come to an end at Urväder Alley, I have nothing but loose gravel ahead of me and I can't go any further. Nor can I go back.

I am left suspended like the victorious Renaissance man in Leonardo's drawing, but am actually quite helpless, incapable of moving either hand or foot from their fragile holds.

The only thing that can save me now is a new ESCARP-MENT – the word itself comes as a great relief and subdues my panic. *If only* the entire universe would tilt like a motorbike on a corner, the centre of gravity would no longer pull me down into death, but would keep me there so that I could slowly crawl up the wall of the house.

Why not? I think. A great many hopes presumed to be the basis of our salvation are less reasonable than that.

93

I drive east towards El Golea. So little happens on this road that each well is marked by its name and depth on the map.

Because each individual moment in the desert is monotonous, it is assumed that it will always go on being monotonous in the same way. That is a mistake. There are a thousand different ways of being monotonous and the desert knows them all.

The emptiness draws you to it like a vacuum. I suddenly remember the smell of wood stacks, and the smell of trains in the days when compartment windows were shut with a leather strap hanging in a dark-brown perforated tongue below the window. And the delicate sound of my father's razor as he stropped the blade . . .

The damp cold in the earth cellar when you enter it to take the muslin covers off the bowls of soured milk. From the musty air in there, I suddenly step out into the warm summer smell of flowers. I close both doors behind me and replace the hasp, which is made of wood. The nettles on both sides of the narrow path are high and menacing. Holding the bowl of soured milk out in front, I hunch up my shoulders and walk between the nettles straight out into summer . . .

In a cloud of memories, I stopped the car at the last of the named wells, *Inhal*, the water in which is said to be '*bonne, abondante, à 12 m*'. Deep down there in the darkness of the well, the surface gleamed, covered in a film of dead insects.

There was neither rope nor chain at the well-head. You are supposed to take your own rope with you. Otherwise you die of thirst by a well of that kind. If you fall in you are lost.

If you fall in . . .

Suddenly I remember the ball, the pail, the rough walls, Edgar and Valter's faces as they disappeared above . . .

Suddenly I remember it all.

94

In my childhood, open wells were common in the Swedish countryside. The water was hauled up in a pail fastened by a rope or a chain to a balancing lever.

All parents warned their children about the well. That was just about as realistic as warning them about the traffic today. When the lid of the well was off, it was strictly forbidden to play by the well. But as soon as we played ball, the ball was drawn in that direction by some mysterious force and often vanished down into the hole. Many a time have I seen the ball floating on the dark gleaming water down there and stood fishing for it with the pail.

When we failed to retrieve it in that way, one of us had to sit on the pail and be lowered down. Edgar was eldest, so went first. Valter was youngest and went down next. The third time, I could hardly refuse.

The Well-divers

I sat on the pail, clutching onto the chain. With a jerk, I shot up in the air when Edgar seized the other end of the lever. Valter grabbed the chain and swung it round towards the well. I hung there slowly twirling above the well opening. My expression must have shown that I was about to burst into tears, had changed my mind and no longer wanted to do this. They stopped for a moment, waiting for me to say something. But I said nothing. Then they began slowly lowering me down the shaft. The longer the chain became between me and Valter, the more the pail spun around, first in one direction, then the other, so that I bounced against the sharp flintstone walls of the well. My hands shook. It was only six or seven metres down to the water, but I daren't look down. Nor did I dare look at the white hole up there growing smaller and smaller and further and further away. Supposing I let go? Supposing I let go! Who would save me down here? It was already too cramped for one person, let alone two. And Valter would never be able to lift both Edgar and me. Now I was down there! My feet and the seat of my trousers were already in the icy water. Now I had to let go with one hand to try and reach the ball. The cramped space suddenly seemed enormous, the ball constantly dancing away. The boys up there tried to move the chain so that I could get nearer the ball. The result was that I swung like a pendulum between the well walls and had to grab the chain with both hands again. I suddenly slipped down half a metre and was seized with panic. I thought I was lost, but they had only ducked me. I still had my head above water. The ball came floating towards me and when I pressed my arms together, it caught in my grip.

'I've got it!' I cried, and they started pulling me up. I sat curled up with the ball against my stomach and chest, twirling around, bouncing through the shaft.

In the Sahara there were wells ten times as deep. In the Sahara it is a profession, the *rtass*'s, descending into wells of that kind and continuing, diving below the surface of the water to clean them out.

95

There is a book of life which can be read in two directions. I read it from the beginning. Then my lips begin to twitch. Quite out of my control, my lips keep trembling against each other. The unpleasant feeling of the actual trembling is made almost unbearable by the sensitive surfaces of my lips rubbing against each other. To relieve it, I try to tremble with my mouth open, but at once it dries up and starts cracking.

Not until I turn the book over and start reading it from the back do my lips grow still and the twitching stops just as suddenly as it had begun.

96

In the low light of the morning sun, I drive between sabre dunes and star dunes on towards Ouargla. The sand trickles and murmurs across the road, like the film of water trickling down the butcher's shop window when I was small.

The entire landscape is based on that contrast: the heavy, firm, dark gravel lying there, sweating desert varnish and being baked together into the rigid base on which the light, bright, mobile sand appears, as fine as pollen and soft as velvet.

Here and there a few sparse twigs of broom are scattered in the sand, sometimes gathered into bushes resembling punk hair styles.

Ouargla has been a town since the sixteenth century. For a long time it was the southernmost post in the French Empire, the starting point for the great Saharan expeditions.

Today, Ouargla is the administrative centre for the oil-rich area of the south. But there are also half a million date palms in the oases and almost as many in the suburbs.

The old houses in Ouargla are built in the characteristic style which in the Sahara goes by the name 'Sudanese'. The material resembles clay, the shapes are soft and organic, the houses apparently growing like fungi or rising like dough. The windows are diagonal slices in the thick fabric of the walls. 'As if the rays of the sun had sliced their way through the walls,' I think – but the cuts are naturally placed counter-clockwise in order to let in as little sun as possible.

At the El Mehri hotel, the starter consists of spaghetti with bread, the main course rice and potatoes. But they play Beethoven's Fifth during the meal and my table napkin is so heavy and moist that when I put it on my lap I can feel the chill right through my clothes.

This dampness is not because the weather in the Sahara isn't good for drying – it is the desert's re-ordering of all values. Damp is the very best. The Sahara has taught me to love the weight and coolness of a really wet table napkin to the sound of Beethoven's Fifth.

After dinner, I go down to the hotel yard as usual for a last check on the car locks and lights. The car park guard has made a small fire of yellow seed-cases and date palm leaves. We start talking.

He was born a *ghattasin*, as the well-divers are called in Ouargla.

'They say we are descendants of prisoners who were sentenced to death. The Turks let them choose between being executed immediately or becoming well-divers in the Sahara. When they came here, they were forced down the wells. But their children and grandchildren were the first to become truly skilled, we who were trained from an early age for this difficult work.

'During the war of liberation, the French tortured their prisoners by holding their heads under water until they almost suffocated. Perhaps you've heard about it? Well, that's also a way of training a child to become a well-diver.

'Many died, so many that the shortage of well-divers threatened to leave the oases deserted.

'"Our children aren't tough enough," the old men said, those who had survived. "May He-who-makes-all-miracles have mercy on us, otherwise the pitiable performance of our children will bury the entire oasis in sand."

'It was the French who saved us from slavery in the wells by their deep drilling. That's also a side of the French Empire that oughtn't to be forgotten.

'The deep bore was first tried in Ghardaia in the late 1890s. They drilled down to 320 metres without finding water.

'The first kilometre-deep borehole was made in Touggourt in 1927, with no result.

'Here in Ouargla, they drilled down just as deeply, again in vain.

'The first successful borehole was made in Zelfana near Ouargla in 1946.

'Like most *ghattasin*, I was trained as a digger as well as a diver. The most dangerous part of digging was the geyser-like eruptions of water which arose when we broke through the sandstone roof at great depths. Here in Ouargla, the water-bearing stratum is under enormous pressure and many *ghattasin* died in accidents of that kind. But in 1946, they stopped digging wells with those risky old methods.

'What remained was the task of cleaning the existing wells. We used tallow to plug our ears and nostrils, and descended to great depths. It was dangerous and painful work with low social status, even lower than the status of the Haratin out-casts. Before we had been praised as the heroes of the oases, but in the days of well-borers, we were no longer as important.

'When the oil began to flow in Hassi Messaoud, many of the *ghattasin* changed identity and became oil workers. It's a less risky and better-paid profession, with high status.

'I myself became a truck driver. I learnt French from the French. I drove the Hassi Messaoud to Constantine route. But I've also driven to places as far away as Insalah and Tammanrasset, and once went to Zinder. I've seen the desert.

'I've had two wives. I have five sons, all employed by the oil company. Now I'm the car park guard here at the hotel. It's a good job for an old man. I look back on an eventful life (*une vie substantielle*). I am glad I survived the horrors of child-hood. I'm glad I didn't have to torment my children in the same way.'

98

The Sahara's water problems appear to have been solved once and for all. Today they bore down to four thousand metres, extracting water which is fifty degrees Celsius. Ouargla is supplied with fifteen thousand litres a minute.

But there is a difference between water and water.

'The water in the wells we used to dig and clean came from self-renewing sources. The fifteen-thousand-litres-a-minute the oases use today are non-renewable. They say it has come trickling through the base rock of the Atlas mountains, two hundred miles north. It has been on its way for thirty-five thousand years.

'So every litre used takes thirty-five thousand years to replace with a new litre of water.

'That worries me. Sometimes I wonder whether the real future profession in the Sahara will be oil-drilling or well-diving.'

99

That is what he said. Now I know. But what I was looking for – where is that?

I haven't dared talk about myself. I am still hiding. I am evading death, the door of childhood and dreams is open only a crack. Almost everything remains.

100

I am small. My hand has five fingers. With them, I hold life in a firm grip.

I grow and my fingers fire shoots. They branch out like cacti. Every branch seems to provide new possibilities. I reach out more, grasp more.

But soon my hand is so full of fingers that they are completely occupied coping with each other. Whatever they are gripping glides away and disappears in the crush.

I realize what is happening and set about thinning out my fingers like carrots in the vegetable garden.

It takes longer than I had calculated. It turns out to be a labour without end.

Then suddenly I am small again. Once more my hand has five fingers.

With them, I take a firm grip on empty air. What I am trying to grasp has come to an end.

Notes

To Tarfaya:
Chet Raymo, *The Crust of our Earth*, Englewood Cliffs, 1983.
Curtis Cate, *Antoine de Saint-Exupéry, His Life and Times*,
  London, 1970.
Antoine de Saint Exupéry, *Oeuvres*, Bibliothèque de la Pléiade,
  1959.
John Mercer, *Spanish Sahara*, London, 1976.
Tony Hodges, *Western Sahara*, Westport USA, 1983

To Smara:
Michel Vieuchange, *Smara the Forbidden City*, London, 1933.

To Laghouat:
Eugène Fromentin, *Un été dans le Sahara*, with introduction
  and notes by Anne-Marie Christin, Paris, 1982.
  Oeuvres complètes, Bibliothèque de la Pléiade, 1984.
James Thompson and Barbara Wright, *La vie et l'oeuvre
  d'Eugène Fromentin*, Paris, 1987.

To Ain Sefra:

Christian Genet, *Pierre Loti – l'enchanteur*, Poitiers, 1988.

Alain Quella-Villéger, *Pierre Loti, l'incompris*, Paris, 1986.

Lesley Blanch, *Pierre Loti, Portrait of an Escapist*, London, 1983.

Isabelle Eberhardt, *Oeuvres complètes* I, Paris, 1988.

Edmonde Charles-Roux, *Un désir d'Orient, la jeunesse d'Isabelle Eberhardt*, Paris, 1988.

Isabelle Eberhardt, *The Passionate Nomad*, London, 1987.

Vagabond, London, 1988.

The Oblivion Seekers, San Francisco, 1982.

Cecily Mackworth, *The Destiny of Isabelle Eberhardt*, New York, 1975, 1986.

Annette Kobak, *Isabelle*, London, 1988.

Lesley Blanch, *The Wilder Shores of Love*, London, 1954, 1984.

The Immoralist:

André Gide, *Romans, Journal 1, Journal 2*, Bibliothèque de la Pléiade.

Pierre de Boisdeffre, *Vie d'André Gide*, Paris, 1970.

Claude Martin, *La maturité d'André Gide*, Paris, 1977.

Yousset Nacib, *Cultures oasiennes, Bou-saada – essai d'histoire sociale*, Algiers, 1986.